T0013071

THE EPIC RETIREMENT BUCKET LIST

THE EPIC

RETIREMENT

BUCKET LIST

150 GLOBE-TROTTING IDEAS
TO INSPIRE YOUR NEXT CHAPTER

JULIE CHICKERY

ROCKRIDGE
PRESS

To my husband, Sean. I couldn't
ask for a better partner.

Thank you for humoring my
whims and making every
adventure special.

As of press time, the URLs in this book link or refer to existing websites on the internet. Rockridge Press is not responsible for the outdated, inaccurate, or incomplete content available on these sites.

Copyright © 2022 by Rockridge Press

All rights reserved. No part of this publication may be reproduced, stored in a retrieval system, or transmitted in any form or by any means, electronic, mechanical, photocopying, recording, scanning, or otherwise, without the prior written permission of the Publisher. Requests to the Publisher for permission should be addressed to the Permissions Department, Rockridge Press, 1955 Broadway, Suite 400, Oakland, CA 94612.

First Rockridge Press trade paperback edition 2022

Rockridge Press and the Rockridge Press logo are trademarks or registered trademarks of Callisto Media Inc. and/or its affiliates in the United States and other countries and may not be used without written permission.

For general information on our other products and services, please contact our Customer Care Department within the United States at (866) 744-2665, or outside the United States at (510) 253-0500.

Paperback ISBN: 978-1-68539-638-1 | eBook ISBN: 979-8-88608-900-4

Manufactured in the United States of America

Interior and Cover Designer: Cat San Juan and Karmen Lizzul
Art Producer: Melissa Malinowsky
Editor: Anna Pulley
Production Editor: Rachel Taenzler
Production Manager: Martin Worthington

Illustrations © Noun Project, pp. xii, 28, 86, 116; all other illustrations used under license from Shutterstock.com

10 9 8 7 6 5 4 3 2 1 0

CONTENTS

Chapter Two: Eat, Drink, and Be Merry 29

Chapter Three: Embrace New Experiences

Chapter Four: Give Back

Chapter Five: Challenge Yourself

Resources

INTRODUCTION

Congratulations on your retirement! You have worked hard for many years, and now is the time to enjoy the fruits of your labor. I'm Julie Chickery, and I'll be your guide as you consider what to do next. After serving twenty years in the U.S. Air Force and an additional ten as a project manager, I joined the ranks of the newly retired looking for fulfilling activities. Over the past five years, I've tried new hobbies, volunteered my talents, and traveled extensively both in the United States and abroad. My husband and I even traveled full-time around the country in a recreational vehicle for a few years.

You are about to embark on the next exciting chapter of your life. You've reached the point where you now have the opportunity to do all of the things you didn't have time to do before. Retirement today is very different than it was for our parents' generation. You're likely younger, healthier, and more active. The world is your oyster, and all you have to do is choose a direction and go.

As you plan, don't feel like you have to lock yourself into any single activity or travel destination. The key is to live a life of purpose and continue to grow as a human being. This is a time of opportunity, exploration, fun, and some well-deserved self-indulgence. You now have the luxury of trying new hobbies, learning more about the world we live in, and, most important, truly experiencing all it has to offer.

Start thinking about where you'd like to travel, what delicacies you'd like to try, and which festivals you want to attend. Throughout this book, I'll share many more options for you to consider. So pull out your bucket list and get ready to add to it!

HOW TO USE THIS BOOK

This book consists of five chapters, each covering a different theme:

- Go Exploring
- Give Back
- Eat, Drink, and Be Merry
- Challenge Yourself
- Embrace New Experiences

Within each chapter, you'll learn about thirty different activities meant to inspire you. Although you may not choose to do every activity, my goal is to offer you plenty of options.

Some will be new hobbies to explore, interests to pursue, and challenges to tackle. The beauty of this layout is that you don't need to read the book in order. You can jump around and focus on the things that really interest you.

Each activity begins with an overview of the experience. If it is travel-related, I'll share highlights about the area. Then I'll provide you with tips and websites for getting started or places to find more information. (Check the Resources on page 147 for longer URLs.) As an example, one of my favorite activities in the "Eat, Drink, and Be Merry" chapter is deep-sea fishing in Key West (page 32). In that activity, I talk about the benefits of that particular location, including recommending a restaurant that will prepare your catch for you.

You can also combine activities from different chapters, particularly if travel is involved. If you've always wanted to go to Switzerland, you can plan to ride the Glacier Express train (page 26) and experience the art of cheesemaking in the Alps (page 37). The suggestions in this book provide maximum flexibility to allow you to make your retirement as unique as you are.

As you begin your new adventure, I'd like to be one of the first to wish you happy and healthy explorations in your retirement!

CHAPTER ONE

GO EXPLORING

One of the greatest gifts of retirement is time to explore. How often have you thought you'd like to visit a destination but didn't have the time needed to fully enjoy it? Now you do! In this chapter, I'll share thirty unique locations and events to explore around the globe. From visiting some of the stunning national parks in the United States to riding horseback on the majestic Kyrgyzstan Steppe, there is something to delight every traveler. Even better, I selected each activity not only to provide an enjoyable destination but also to help you continue to find wonders in the world around you.

Walk among Giants

For a truly magical experience, walk among the tallest trees in the world at Redwood National and State Parks in Northern California. Towering high above the rocky coastline, these trees can reach heights greater than 300 feet—taller than a thirty-story skyscraper! Start with a scenic drive to get the lay of the land. Then enjoy an intimate encounter with the parks' natural beauty as you stroll through the old-growth forests carpeted with lush ferns below and the majestic redwood trees high above. With more than 200 miles of hiking trails, there is something for everyone, from short jaunts to more challenging treks.

Get started! Find the best outdoor activities for you on the website (nps.gov/redw/planyourvisit) or at any of the five visitor centers located throughout the parks.

――――――― 2 ―――――――

See Salmon Run in Seattle

Each year, the rivers and creeks in the Pacific Northwest come alive with thousands of salmon as they make their way from the ocean into freshwater rivers to spawn. Imagine the New York City subway at rush hour—only it's a river boiling with fish, a phenomenon that has occurred for thousands of years. The Ballard Locks in Seattle, Washington have a twenty-one-step fish ladder with glass windows to allow underwater viewing and are a popular destination to view the action. The visitor center also has great exhibits.

Get started! The Seattle Aquarium provides trained naturalists at several sites along the Cedar River to help the public learn more about the significance of the salmon run. Find out where and when they'll be available at seattleaquarium.org/salmon-journey.

Explore an Exotic Rain Forest

With more than half of the country covered in rain forest, it's no wonder Costa Rica is often referred to as the "jewel of Central America." Explore these diverse ecosystems by hiking through the jungle, zip-lining through the treetops, or even taking a canopy tour. Costa Rica is home to an estimated 500,000 species of plants and animals, many of which can't be found anywhere else on the planet. While visiting, you can expect to see an amazing array of plant and animal life, including monkeys, sloths, toucans, and butterflies.

Get started! For the best of both worlds, plan a trip to Corcovado National Park. It boasts abundant nature trails along both inland and coastal routes, so you can experience the beach and jungle from one destination.

Luxuriate in Dubai's Island Vibes

For a unique beach destination that can't be matched, look no further than Palm Jumeirah, an elaborate man-made island made to look like a palm tree from the air. With several different land masses, it is an astonishing artificial archipelago that added thirty-five miles to the country's coastline. Looking down from one of the towering skyscrapers offers a unique perspective on how humans can alter the natural world. During your visit, enjoy all the luxury Dubai has become known for, from high-end resorts to world-class dining. If you're looking for a great place to stay, consider the Atlantis resort with several restaurants, a massive aquarium, and more.

Get started! See what all the fuss is about as you enjoy a virtual tour of this marvel of modern engineering at airpano.com /360photo/uae-dubai-islands-virtual-tour.

Cruise Down the Mighty Mississippi

For an alternative to a road trip, consider a river trip on a traditional paddlewheel boat! American Cruise Lines offers four authentic replica paddlewheelers with modern amenities and private balconies sailing with a range of itineraries on the Mississippi, America's second-largest river. Go big by choosing the twenty-two-day cruise from Baton Rouge, Louisiana, to St. Paul, Minnesota. Along the way, you'll enjoy culinary delights prepared by the onboard chef, learn about American history with lectures given by historians, and see the stunning landscapes that inspired Mark Twain.

Get started! Peruse photos of the ships and choose the itinerary that best suits your desires at americancruiselines.com/usa -riverboat-cruise-ships/authentic-paddlewheelers-cruise-ships.

Island-Hop around Indonesia

With 17,000 islands, there is no shortage of sun-soaked destinations to enjoy in Indonesia. Bali is the best-known Indonesian island and is a great start to your island-hopping adventure. Bali offers so much more than the stunning beaches you've probably seen in photos. You can raft on the Ayung River, explore picturesque waterfalls, snorkel the Coral Triangle, and tour ancient Hindu temples. From Bali, you can easily get to other islands like Gili Trawangan, Lombok, and Flores, where you'll feel worlds away from the hustle and bustle of the modern world.

Get started! The best time to visit is during September and October, when the weather is dry but there are fewer crowds. Use this trip planner to customize your visit: inspirock.com/indonesia -trip-planner.

Road-Trip through Utah's Mighty Five

A road trip is arguably the best way to experience one of the United States' greatest wonders, Utah's five national parks: Arches, Canyonlands, Capitol Reef, Bryce Canyon, and Zion. And the best way to do it? Combine your lodging with your vehicle by renting a recreational vehicle. You'll have the choice of camping in the national parks or luxury RV resorts along the way. A 935-mile round-trip drive from Salt Lake City will take you to the iconic parks known as the Mighty Five.

Start at Arches National Park, where rangers offer a guided two-and-half-hour tour through the mazelike Fiery Furnace. Of course, no visit would be complete without an up-close view of the world-famous Delicate Arch.

Roll on to Canyonlands, the most rugged and remote of the five parks, which is perfect for a 4x4 or jeep tour.

Make Capitol Reef your next stop to take a glimpse of the area's homesteading past. To this day, you can pick from the historic orchards of the Fruita pioneer community.

Move two hours south to Bryce Canyon, best known for its impressive hoodoos, which are unusual rock formations shaped by erosion. Drive from the visitor center to fifteen different vantage points to get the full experience.

Finish up your adventure at Zion, which boasts two famous hikes, the Narrows and Angels Landing, and bucket list activities for explorers worldwide.

Get started! Rent an RV through outdoorsy.com, which pairs private owners with travelers. It provides you with the most options, from small van-style campers to large motor homes and everything in between.

Traverse the Cabot Trail

The Cabot Trail, a scenic highway on Nova Scotia's Cape Breton Island, boasts some very dramatic landscapes. Over the 185-mile drive, you can marvel at the beauty of rocky coastlines, the wooded Margaree River Valley, and the Bras d'Or Lakes region. Travelers in search of a challenge can even bike the Cabot Trail. Regardless of your mode of transportation, there are plenty of opportunities to be active along the way.

Baddeck is a great starting point for your journey. Home to the Alexander Graham Bell National Historic Site, it's a great place to wander through the world's largest collection of his scientific work and enjoy the views at his summer home, Beinn Bhreagh. From Baddeck, you can also sail on a charter around its large saltwater lake, also known as an inland sea.

Once you set out on the Cabot Trail, your first stop will be in the Margaree River Valley, known for excellent fly-fishing. Find out more by visiting the Margaree Salmon Museum or the fish hatchery to learn about the salmon and trout restocking programs.

Moving on, you'll approach the Acadian coastline and French-speaking village of Chéticamp. This is a great stop to enjoy a pilot whale–watching cruise before embarking on the highlight of the Cabot Trail: Cape Breton Highlands National Park. At this park, you'll walk through breathtaking headland cliffs, idyllic coves, and sandy beaches.

Get started! Fly into McCurdy Sydney airport and rent a car for the 245-mile road trip. Plan your lodging and sightseeing trips at https://cabottrail.travel.

Pay Tribute to Fallen Heroes

Located on the northern coast of France, the beaches along the fifty-mile stretch of Normandy coast are best known as the location where D-Day unfolded during World War II. There were five beach landing points on D-Day: Omaha, Utah, Gold, Juno, and Sword beaches, where Allied soldiers gave their lives to help end Europe's Nazi occupation. Americans stormed Omaha, Utah, and Gold, while British troops fought at Sword and Canadian soldiers at Juno.

Begin your visit at the Bayeux War Cemetery, where 4,144 Commonwealth soldiers are buried. The Bayeux Memorial opposite the cemetery lists the names of an additional 1,800 soldiers who died during the fighting but have no known grave. Just over ten miles away is the Normandy American Cemetery, the final resting place of 9,400 Americans. At the cemetery, you can also wander among the chapel, monuments, and a twenty-two-foot bronze statue.

From there, make your way to Omaha Beach. In 2004, the sculpture *Les Braves* was erected here to honor the bravery of the Allied soldiers. Gaze out toward the sea where soldiers landed, and don't forget to turn your head toward the towering bluffs where the Germans rained fire down upon them.

Sword Beach is home to a museum housed in a German bunker. Also offered are guided tours of bunkers and tunnels leading to an underground command post at Juno Beach.

Get started! There are dozens of museums and memorials dedicated to that fateful day, with the Memorial Museum of the Battle of Normandy in Bayeux the most comprehensive. Learn more at bayeuxmuseum.com/en.

Pedal through the Petals

Known for its canals, multicolored tulip fields, and windmills, the Netherlands is famously picturesque. Add its relatively flat topography, safe bicycle lanes, and numerous rental options, and you have a biking destination made in heaven.

Each spring the Bollenstreek, or bulb region, comes alive with tulips. At its heart is Keukenhof park, where more than seven million tulip bulbs are planted annually. You can visit from Amsterdam by taking a bus to the park and renting a bike when you arrive. The park has four routes for a self-guided tour of five, ten, fifteen, or twenty-five kilometers around their flower fields. Be sure to allow time for a stroll around the seventy-nine-acre gardens.

As a special treat, if you are in the area the third week of April, attend the Bloemencorso Bollenstreek. This flower festival lasts a week and culminates in a twenty-six-mile-long parade that runs through several villages, most of which have local activities throughout the day. The elaborate floats are decorated with colorful hyacinths, daffodils, and tulips.

Also consider booking a multiday tour: Holland Bike Tours offers a four-day one covering about 12.5 miles a day. (You can even rent an e-bike, if you prefer.) In addition to Keukenhof and numerous flower fields, the tour includes a stop at the world's largest flower market in Aalsmeer, where more than twenty million flowers are sold every day.

Get started! Keukenhof park (keukenhof.nl/en) is only open during the tulip season between mid-March and mid-May, with the peak in mid-April, so be sure to time your visit accordingly.

Follow in Darwin's Footsteps

The Galápagos Islands are well-known for their pristine environment, crystal-clear waters, and fascinating history. Another highlight of the islands is the diversity of wildlife, much of which cannot be found anywhere else in the world—which is what drew famed naturalist Charles Darwin.

As a young explorer, Darwin joined an expedition to the archipelago on the HMS *Beagle*. Over five weeks, he spent time on the following four islands making observations that ultimately formed the basis of his seminal work *On the Origin of Species.*

San Cristóbal, home to the capital of the archipelago, was the first island Darwin visited. He was surprised that it consisted of rocky lava rather than a tropical landscape.

Although Floreana was the first populated island, fewer than 200 people live there today. The big draw for visitors is the unique snorkeling opportunities of the Devil's Crown, a submerged volcanic crater.

Isabela is one of the only places in the world where you can see both flamingos and penguins. The Galápagos penguin is the second smallest of its kind in the world. A major draw of Isabela island is the thousands of Galápagos tortoises living on the island's volcanic slopes.

Perhaps no island is more desired by bird lovers than Santiago. Its rocky cliffs form the perfect nesting site for hundreds of marine birds.

Get started! A cruise is the best way to visit the Galápagos if you want to be able to visit more than just one or two islands. Hurtigruten Expeditions (hurtigruten.com) has a nine-day itinerary that traces Darwin's steps.

Venture under the Sea

The Great Barrier Reef is great for a reason: It's the world's largest marine ecosystem, consisting of more than 3,000 coral reefs as well as 300 coral cays, 600 islands, and 150 mangrove islands. It's so large—about half the size of Texas—that you can easily find snorkeling tours from several locations on Australia's east coast. If you really want to fully immerse yourself in the wonders of the reef, you can also stay on one of the islands. Fitzroy Island offers visitors the choice of a luxury resort or more budget-friendly camping options. You can take a boat tour to different parts of the reef or snorkel right from the beach whenever you want.

Regardless of where you launch your snorkeling adventure, once you submerge yourself in the clear water, you will be amazed by the colors of the marine plants and coral. Even more exciting to most visitors is the chance to swim with the many species of rays, sharks, turtles, and whales. And we can't forget the fish. As the reef is home to more than 1,600 species of fish, you'll see every type you can imagine!

Be sure to pay a visit to the unique Museum of Underwater Art. It features a number of submerged sculptures made from eco-friendly materials that provide homes for marine life. Divers have the best view, but snorkelers can see them from above.

Get started! Plan your trip for specific times of the year if you're interested in specific marine life encounters. For example, the dwarf minke whale migration occurs each June and July.

Swim in a Cave

The Yucatán Peninsula in southeastern Mexico is known for its Mayan ruins, crystal-clear waters, and lush jungles with thousands of cenotes. A cenote is a limestone sinkhole that is filled with water, creating gorgeous underground swimming holes. When you enter the splendor of a grand cenote with turquoise pools and vibrant plants along the walls, you understand why they were sacred to the ancient Mayans.

Today, many cenotes have been modified to include ladders and platforms around the edges for swimmers to rest on after their dips. Many tour operators offer cenote excursions so you don't have to worry about transportation.

Tulum is home to Parque Nacional Tulum, an archaeological site with white sandy beaches and several cenotes. From the well-known cavernous Gran Cenote to the more open Cenote Zacil-Ha, there are options for everyone.

Gran Cenote's proximity to the Tulum ruins is only one of the reasons for its popularity. Swimmers and divers love exploring the network of caverns and its large cave with stalactites. If you don't like enclosed spaces, you can enjoy the crystalline waters surrounded by the jungle in the open-air cenote.

Cenote Zacil-Ha is a great choice if you're looking for a completely open swimming pool–style cenote. Adventurous souls can even choose to zip-line and drop into it!

Get started! Tulum is a great home base for your visit: It's only a ninety-minute drive south of the Cancún airport, but it is more relaxed and focused on ecotourism. As an added bonus, it is close to many cenotes.

Summit Sicily's Volcano

Have you ever wondered what it would be like to stand on an active volcano? If so, consider Sicily, home to Mount Etna, one of the tallest active volcanoes in Europe, standing at just under 11,000 feet above sea level. The Sapienza Refuge on the southern side of the volcano is the best way to get there.

The trip to the summit is a lot of fun in itself. First, you take the Funivia dell'Etna cable car from the refuge to 2,500 meters (8,200 feet) elevation. On the way up, you'll enjoy a bird's-eye view of the surrounding landscape. Then you transfer to a four-wheel-drive Unimog bus that will take you to the lower crater area. (There was another cable car station at that point, but it was melted by an eruption!) From there, you can look around the lower craters or continue with a guide to the highest craters near the summit. Visitors often say the barren landscape reminds them of the moon's surface.

Don't forget to visit the often-overlooked northern side of Mount Etna, with a much different type of landscape. In the spring and summer, it has a vibrant forest with wildflowers, and you can even ski on the volcano in the winter. The northern side also has several lava tubes, or caves created by lava flow.

Get started! Etna 3340 (etna3340.com/en) offers several excursions on and around the volcano. From a challenging summit hike to a twilight trek, there's something for everyone.

Witness a Wildebeest Migration

For an unforgettable African safari, you're not going to want to miss the largest mammal migration on earth. This truly spectacular experience occurs each year when millions of wildebeests and herds of grazing animals like gazelles and zebras move through the Serengeti in a circular pattern following the rainfall and green pastures. The movement of these animals also increases your chance of seeing their predators, like cheetahs, hyenas, leopards, and lions.

Serengeti National Park is located in north-central Tanzania. It is a protected wildlife refuge for the animals previously mentioned, in addition to crocodiles, elephants, giraffes, hippopotamuses, and rhinoceroses. The park is also a bird lover's paradise, with more than 350 species of birds, from pygmy falcons to ostriches and everything in between.

A great option to ensure you have the best chance of witnessing this spectacle is to book your trip with a mobile camp like the Nomad Serengeti Safari Camp, which moves throughout the year based on the location of the herds. This isn't rugged camping; think luxury tents with private bathrooms. Each evening, you can expect sunset dinners and drinks. Most safari operators and lodges partner with locals for perishable foods, so you can expect meals with seasonal ingredients and regional touches.

Get started! Timing and flexibility are key when it comes to maximizing your potential to see the especially big herds. Late January to early February is calving season and the optimal time to see larger herds together. If you're trying to catch the hordes crossing the Mara River, your best bet is early summer.

Seek the Lost City of Petra

Channel your inner Indiana Jones to witness the remains of ancient civilization firsthand. Famous for the scene where Jones finds the Holy Grail, ancient Petra is an authentic remnant of the past. The impressive city stretches over 102 square miles, all carved into sandstone cliffs. Located in modern-day Jordan, about a three-hour drive from Amman, Petra was the capital of the Nabataean kingdom from the first century BCE until it was largely abandoned in the eighth century CE.

Although archaeologists have only excavated about 15 percent of the original site, numerous buildings are exceptionally well preserved, providing visitors with much to explore. Many choose to visit for more than one day to take it all in.

The entrance to Petra is through the Siq, a towering passage between two rock walls that is three-quarters of a mile long. Once you pass through the Siq, you'll come face-to-face with The Treasury, or Al-Khazneh. Standing at more than forty meters (131 feet) high, this impressive facade is the most photographed in Petra. Continuing on the two-and-half-mile main trail along the colonnaded street, you'll encounter the Hellenic-style amphitheater and the royal tombs.

Get started! The main trail is always the most crowded, so if you have time to take one or two of the other trails, you'll have more space to enjoy the sites. It will take a bit of stamina, but if you can hike about four miles round-trip and climb several hundred steps up to the High Place of Sacrifice, you'll get a phenomenal view from above the city. (visitpetra.jo)

Brave the Drake Passage to Antarctica

Yes, you can visit Antarctica, and the best way to do it is on an authentic expedition cruise ship. Extending from South America's southernmost tip to Antarctica's South Shetland Islands, the 600-mile Drake Passage serves as the shortest route to the icy continent. As you move through the passage, you can take time to reflect on the intrepid explorers who were there first. Although the English name comes from Sir Francis Drake, he was not the first to pass through. The first was Spanish navigator Francisco de Hoces in 1525, and Spanish maps identify the passage as Mar de Hoces.

On your journey, you'll have a front-row seat to the dramatic blue-hued icebergs as the ship makes its way toward the northern peninsula. Excursions on small Zodiac (inflatable) boats through ice-choked channels are a highlight for most Antarctic cruisers. Some cruises even offer guided kayak tours!

Regardless of your mode of transportation, you are sure to see seals, whales, and penguin rookeries with thousands of these flight-less birds. Another highlight for travelers to Antarctica is the sight of Deception Island. An active volcano, it doesn't have snow in many places, which makes it a stark contrast to the rest of the area.

Get started! When booking your cruise, pay close attention to the itinerary if you actually want to set foot in Antarctica. Many cruises merely sail around it. The *National Geographic Explorer* has a fourteen-day cruise that includes the Drake Passage, the chance to walk on the continent, and much more.

Trek the Great Wall of China

At 13,170 miles, the Great Wall is the longest structure ever built. What many people don't realize is that it started as separate walls beginning in the seventh century BCE through the Ming Dynasty (1368–1644). Another interesting fact is that not all portions of the wall are in the great condition you might see in photos. The sections around Beijing and a few other tourist hubs are fully renovated and are even accessible to wheelchair users, but many other portions are referred to as "wild." You can still walk on them, but they are more challenging.

Badaling and Mutianyu outside Beijing are the two most popular sections of the wall for tourists. Mutianyu was fully restored to replicate the Ming Dynasty fortifications. From the main entry, you can walk up to the wall or ride a cable car to get an aerial view. From there, experience the thrill of walking on the Great Wall of China through watchtowers, reveling in the spectacular vistas of forests and mountains.

If you'd like a more strenuous tour to experience parts both restored and wild, walk the six miles from Mutianyu to Jiankou, the steepest section. Once you are beyond tower twenty-three, there are no guardrails, and you will experience parts that are crumbling.

Get started! Beijing is a great base for your Great Wall exploration. Both Badaling and Mutianyu are within forty-five miles of the city. If you're not going with a tour group, Badaling is the most accessible by bus, metro, or even a bullet train that will get you there in twenty minutes.

Canoe to the World's Tallest Waterfall

Niagara Falls who? If you want to see a real waterfall, travel to south-eastern Venezuela to Angel Falls, the world's tallest waterfall. Almost twenty times taller than Niagara Falls, it drops from the steep face of a *tepui*, or flat-top mountain. Located in the remote Canaima National Park, the trip is an adventure in itself.

Start with a flight from Caracas to Canaima, where you can explore the Canaima Lagoon area. Next, you'll board a *curiara*, or motorized canoe, for a six-hour ride along the river before arriving at Devil's Canyon, where you can see the majestic waterfall from a distance. The final leg is a one-hour hike through the jungle to reach the base of the falls. After relaxing in the pools of the falls, you can explore nearby caves and hiking trails. Depending on the tour you book, you'll return to Canaima Lagoon that day or stay the night in a hammock in front of the falls.

Osprey Expeditions is a highly rated tour operator that offers trips to the park from Caracas. Trips typically include a couple of days in the Canaima Lagoon area exploring other waterfalls, hiking through the jungle, swimming in the lake, and experiencing the culture of an Indigenous village.

Get started! Another fabulous option is to stay at the Waku Lodge at Canaima Lagoon. You can get full packages that include your flight, Angel Falls tour, and other excursions in the park, including a flight over the falls to get an aerial view.

Stand atop a Rock Fortress

Originally a palace for King Kashyapa (477–495 CE) on a rock column towering 600 feet above the countryside, Sigiriya is now a UNESCO World Heritage site and one of the top places to visit in Sri Lanka. Sigiriya is also called Lion Rock for the large rock sculptures of lion paws you will pass through on the 1,200-step climb. It takes forty-five minutes to an hour for most travelers to ascend, with many points of interest along the way to allow you time to recover. The three distinct gardens highlight why the complex is recognized as the earliest example of urban planning. At the top, explore the Cobra Hood Cave, home to fresco paintings more than 1,700 years old.

Get started! Stay at the thirty-two-acre Aliya Resort with views of Lion Rock from your room. (themeresorts.com/aliyaresort)

Drive Sky-High

Most of Colorado's fourteeners (summits over 14,000 feet above sea level) are only accessible by challenging hikes. Luckily, you can take a thrilling drive to the 14,115-foot summit of Pikes Peak near Colorado Springs. For nineteen miles, follow Pikes Peak Highway, with 156 turns through aspen and pine forests. Once you reach the summit, immerse yourself in the exhibits at the visitor center. Don't forget to try an altitude donut, the only donuts made above 14,000 feet. There are several stops to enjoy the beauty of Pike National Forest. You can even pan for gold, explore nature trails, and trout fish.

Get started! If you'd like to experience the drive without your hands behind the wheel, get a ride on the Pikes Peak Cog Railway, the highest of its kind in the world. (cograilway.com)

Wander in an Artful Garden

Covering just over eleven acres, the Villa d'Este gardens in Tivoli, Italy, are a true wonderland, recognized by UNESCO as a model for gardens all over Europe. The palace and gardens were designed by famed architect Pirro Ligorio to be a work of art, and that intention shows in every detail.

Allow yourself plenty of time to take in the details of the hundreds of water features, including grottos, pools, and waterfalls. These water displays were built in the sixteenth century and are completely powered by gravity, making them an engineering marvel, too. Although every detail is exquisite, the fountains are the true masterpieces here, with three being the most well known.

First, in the center of the upper garden is the Fountain of the Dragons, showcasing rock sculptures and waterworks. It's framed by two semicircular ramps that create a dramatic effect. The Fountain of the Organ is one of the most photographed. Built in 1566 by Luc Leclerc, it was the first of its kind, with an elaborate system of 144 pipes and a water-powered mechanism that creates the sound of an organ. Finally, down a path known as the Avenue of a Hundred Fountains, you'll arrive at the Oval Fountain (Fontana dell'Ovato). It looks like an elaborate semicircle-shaped waterfall complete with a rocky mountain rising up behind it.

Get started! The gardens are located just twenty miles east of Rome, and you can take a train to Tivoli and a quick shuttle bus to the gardens, allowing you to spend as much time as you like contemplating the beauty around you.

Climb inside a Glacier

Walking through crystal-blue glacier caves is a surreal experience—sort of like walking under a frozen ocean. Glaciers actually only exist on land, but they do often have an adjacent lagoon formed from meltwater. The only way to experience these caves is through a guided tour, and the best place to do it is at Vatnajökull glacier in Iceland.

An interesting fact to note is that these glaciers are constantly moving. Rivers also run under the glaciers in the summer, reshaping them, so if you see photos of an ice cave from last season, it will likely be different the following year. During some seasons, you can't even access caves that were accessible in previous years, which is one of the reasons experienced guides are necessary. Each season, they identify the safest caves for tour groups. One cave that has been accessible for a decade is the Crystal Cave. Due to its large size, summer melt has merely reformed it rather than completely erasing it.

Glacier cave accessibility is weather dependent. The prime season is mid-October through March. If you can't visit Iceland during that time, the man-made tunnels at Langjökull are a great alternative. They were formed higher on the glacier, which makes them more stable throughout the year.

Get started! Since Vatnajökull glacier is more than 200 miles from the airport at Reykjavik, the best way to experience the caves is through a two- or three-day tour of Iceland's South Coast. These tours typically add activities like hiking on top of glaciers.

Horse-Trek to Kyrgyzstan Steppes

If you are looking for a completely different tourist experience, this one is for you! By going on a tour, you can experience the life of a nomad on the Kyrgyzstan steppes. Some background: Kyrgyzstan is a country in central Asia with incredible natural beauty, and a steppe is a dry, grassy plain in an area that gets less than twenty inches of rain a year. It is perfect for grazing animals and, thus, supports the lives of nomadic herders.

The people of the steppe have struggled to maintain their traditions, but horses are an integral part of their daily existence and the perfect way for you to tour the area. A typical horseback tour consists of three to four hours of riding a day for several days. You'll stay in traditional yurts as well as village inns.

Starting from the capital city of Bishkek, you'll ride to Issyk-Kul, a saline lake surrounded by snow-capped peaks. Issyk-Kul means "warm lake," and the name is very fitting, as the saline content keeps the lake from freezing in even the coldest temperatures. It was originally a stop on the Silk Road trade route, and archaeologists have found the remnants of a large city at the bottom of it.

A highlight of the tour is an eagle hunting demonstration. The hunters, called *berkutchi*, capture wild golden eagles to train for small-game hunting. Other demonstrations to look for are yurt building, felt making, and local cooking.

Get started! Tripaneer has several guided tours in Kyrgyzstan with itineraries from six to fourteen days, suitable for a wide range of horseback-riding experience.

Travel through Time

More than just a quaint European destination, historic Warsaw is a testament to the indomitable spirit of the Polish people. The city was intentionally razed by Nazi Germany in late 1944 as an act of reprisal for the Polish resistance. Engineers and demolition teams were sent throughout the city to burn and dynamite anything in their paths. They especially focused on destroying important historical buildings, churches, and libraries.

For five years after the war, citizens worked diligently to reconstruct the old town. These efforts are recognized in the UNESCO World Heritage List for authentically restoring the city's late-eighteenth-century appearance. The blueprints that were used for the reconstruction efforts are very interesting: They're paintings! Italian painter Bernardo Bellotto was a court painter to the king of Poland in 1768 and created *vedutes*, or large-scale, realistic paintings of the city.

A great place to start your tour through the cobblestone streets of Warsaw is the Old Town Market Place. Once the center of public life, it now houses the Museum of Warsaw. The Royal Castle was furnished with repossessed furniture and art originally stolen by the Nazis. One new addition next to the ramparts of Old Town is a monument in honor of the child soldiers of the Warsaw Uprising. The statue *Maly Powstaniec*, or *The Little Insurrectionist*, is of a young boy wearing an oversized helmet.

For a food-and-drinks-based Poland adventure, see page 47.

Get started! Housed inside the historic Mokrowsky Palace, the Mamaison Hotel Le Regina is the perfect place to stay while visiting the historic Old Town.

Traverse the Great Silk Road

This collection of ancient trade routes is a UNESCO World Heritage site that stretches for more than 6,000 miles from China to the Mediterranean Sea. Today, travelers can trace its path exploring an incredible diversity of cultures, religions, and landscapes. Originating in China, goods traveled overland to present-day Istanbul before being shipped up the Mediterranean to Europe. The name comes from the silk textiles that were highly desired in Egypt, Greece, and Rome.

In China, the Silk Road begins in the city of Xi'an, home to the Terracotta Army of the Qin dynasty. From there, the route passes through the Taklamakan Desert past the intricate cave dwellings of Dunhuang to the oasis town of Turpan. Kashgar was a major hub with both northern and southern routes converging there. The livestock market of the Ivan Bazaar still functions as one of the region's largest. Farther west, the Silk Road winds through snow-capped mountains and barren steppes before skirting the Black and Caspian seas on the way to the Mediterranean. Trade was active for about 1,500 years, until the rise of the Ottoman Empire put an end to it. Throughout its history, the Silk Road has been a conduit for trade and cultural exchange, and now it offers visitors a window into that rich past.

Get started! History buffs can now take an epic forty-eight-day guided journey across six countries to travel the primary route. The guided tour uses a combination of boats, buses, flights, and trains to make the trek through China, Kyrgyzstan, Uzbekistan, Turkmenistan, Iran, and Turkey.

Visit a Vanishing Wonder

Did you know that Glacier National Park is home to twenty-five glaciers? It sounds impressive until you learn that, when the park was created in 1910, there were more than one hundred. Scientists estimate that all of the park's glaciers will be gone within the next few decades. As a result, it is more important than ever to visit Glacier National Park while it still exists in its current form.

Located in northwest Montana, the glaciers are just the tip of the iceberg when it comes to the natural beauty of Glacier National Park. It's also home to numerous alpine meadows, more than 700 lakes, 200 waterfalls, and 150 mountain peaks. From boating and fishing to hiking and attending ranger-led nature walks, there is truly no limit to the activities it offers. Wildlife viewing is always a draw for national parks, and Glacier is no exception. The area has bears (grizzly and black), bighorn sheep, cougars, elk, mountain goats, river otters, and more.

The scenic Going-to-the-Sun Road is a highlight for park visitors. It spans fifty miles and crosses the Continental Divide at Logan Pass. You'll get a front-seat view of all the park has to offer. However, it is a narrow two-lane road with steep drop-offs and can be stressful for the driver. That said, the park does offer a free shuttle service.

Get started! If you're trying to choose a time to visit, consider this: The summer is exceptionally busy. Plan a visit during late September and early October. The only thing you'll risk missing out on is the higher elevations of the Going-to-the-Sun Road. (nps.gov/glac)

Saddle Up for Morocco's Desert

Camels have played a central role in the North African desert for thousands of years. They've traditionally been used as mode of transportation for both people and goods across a vast and unforgiving landscape. Today, many visitors to Morocco take camel rides through the desert, enjoying the unique experience of traversing the sand dunes on these iconic animals.

The portion of the Sahara Desert closest to Marrakech is actually rocky and flat. If you're envisioning a classic camel trek among sand dunes but are afraid of spending too much time in the saddle, consider a three-day tour from Marrakech to Fès. The first day of travel will be by bus or jeep across the Atlas Mountains to Ait-Ben-Haddou, where you can tour a traditional pre-Saharan habitat. The second day of the journey is when you'll join the camel caravan to experience the towering Erg Chebbi dunes that can reach heights of over 500 feet. That night, you'll enjoy an authentic dinner under the stars and sleep in a Bedouin camp in the desert. On day three, you'll return to Marrakech by bus or jeep with a stop in Ouarzazate to wander around the Taourirt Kasbah, where many Hollywood films were set.

Learn about Moroccan food and cooking on page 38.

Get started! The influx of tourism to the region has many wondering if it is ethical to ride camels during your travels. As with any animal encounter, the most important things you can do as a responsible tourist are read reviews, research ethical tour operators, and observe handlers for humane treatment.

Hop aboard Switzerland's Famed Rail

For a great overview of the Swiss Alps, consider a trip on the famed Glacier Express train traveling between St. Moritz and Zermatt at the base of the Matterhorn. If you are riding straight through, the full journey will take about eight hours. The train traverses ninety-one tunnels and crosses 291 bridges as it makes its way through narrow valleys and rocky gorges. One of the best upgrades you can get is for the premium luxury car called "excellence class." You'll be served wine and a seven-course meal prepared with locally sourced ingredients. Every seat offers a window view, providing you with a full day's visual appreciation of the Swiss Alps.

As you might imagine, this journey is all about the scenery. Beginning at the base of the famed Matterhorn mountain in Zermatt, you'll travel through the heart of the Alps as the train rolls up and down from alpine valleys to the Oberalp Pass, the line's high point at 6,670 feet above sea level. Throughout the journey, you'll experience incredibly diverse landscapes with glaciers, valleys, forests, and meadows that will call to you for a closer look. Luckily, that is easy to do in this country with the highest rail usage in the world.

Pair your rail adventure with other Swiss expeditions on page 37 and 81.

Get started! Although the word "express" is in the title, the train is not fast. If there are places along the way you want to visit, the best option is to use traditional trains on your return trip. Plan your railway excursion through the Alps at glacierexpress.ch/en.

Soak in a Volcanic Hot Tub

Aso-Kuju National Park is home to some of the most stunning scenery in all of Japan. From its picturesque lakes and rivers to its volcanic landscapes, the park offers visitors a chance to experience the country's natural beauty firsthand. And one of the best ways to enjoy the park is by soaking in the hot springs at Yufuin Onsen. The streets are lined with inns, or ryokan, and public bath houses where you can take a soak. The hot springs are renowned for their therapeutic benefits, and their tranquil setting makes them the perfect place to relax and rejuvenate after a day exploring the park.

Located on the island of Kyushu, Aso-Kuju National Park is best known for Mount Aso, the largest active volcano in Japan. At seventy-four miles in circumference, the Aso caldera is one of the largest in the world. A great way to get your first look is by driving up the Milk Road to Daikanbo. This is the highest point on the northern caldera edge, and it provides spectacular views.

The Kuju Mountain Range offers fabulous hiking opportunities. Both the Makinoto Pass and Chojabaru Visitor Center are easily accessible from the main drive and have major trailheads. Mount Nakadake, the park's highest point, rises 5,875 feet above sea level. Its crater is filled with a bright blue pool that often has steam rising from it.

For other Japan experiences, check out page 30 and page 33.

Get started! Reach the island via a short flight (under two hours) from Tokyo. You'll enjoy the slower-paced island life after visiting the big city.

CHAPTER TWO

EAT, DRINK, AND BE MERRY

Retirement is a time to celebrate, and what better way to do it than with the finest food and drinks? In this chapter, you'll find some of the best culinary delights around the world. We all know that the right cuisine can enhance any experience. If you're visiting Japan, why not have fresh sushi prepared in front of you? Love wine? Consider taking a sommelier course in South Africa or stomping grapes in California. By embarking on these culinary journeys from fine dining to street food, you'll expand your worldview as you expand your palate.

Watch Tokyo's Famed Tuna Auction

For a truly unique experience, a visit to Tokyo's famed fish market Toyosu should be on your agenda. Here, you can get a great view of the tuna auction and watch buyers compete each morning for the best tuna. It's a fascinating, fast-paced show. After the auction, wander the rest of the complex where more than a hundred eateries and shops vie for your business. Don't leave without trying the sushi. Skip the menu and ask for the omakase, or chef's pick of the day.

Get started! Watch the auction from the elevated viewing area. Look for the Language Volunteer Co-talk jackets for helpful folks who can answer questions in English.

Try Romantic Raft Dining in Zambia

After a day of exploring the Zambian landscapes and Victoria Falls, there's nothing better than enjoying dinner while basking in the warm glow of a beautiful sunset. At the Tongabezi Lodge, you can savor your meal from a *sampan*, or floating platform, *on* the Zambezi River! As you delight in your surroundings with a bottle of local wine, servers in canoes deliver traditional cuisine right to you. Their chefs offer dynamic seasonal menus based on fresh, locally sourced ingredients to provide you with an authentic culinary experience. The sindambi (a wild hibiscus) and sage-glazed roasted pork belly is a star of the menu.

Get started! As you can imagine, this private dinner for two is in high demand. Visit greensafaris.com to make your sampan dining reservation.

Stomp Like Lucy in Napa Valley

If you love wine, take it a step further and participate in the ancient art of grape stomping in Napa Valley, California. Ever since Mike Grgich stunned wine elites by besting famous French labels in the 1976 Judgment of Paris wine competition, Napa Valley has been recognized as a leader in world-class wines. Grgich Hills Estate winery, with its five vineyards over 366 acres, offers the opportunity to jump in a barrel of fresh-picked grapes each day during the harvest.

Get started! The annual harvest occurs between August and October. Wear shorts, a skirt, or pants that can easily be rolled up to participate in this fun experience. (grgich.com/grape-stomping)

34

Be Your Family's Betty Crocker

Now that you're retired, you finally have time to preserve all the family recipes you loved as a child in a cookbook. The food and beverages we enjoy at special holiday meals and family gatherings tell a story about us. In many cases, these recipes have been handed down for generations. As you start brainstorming which recipes to include, think of beloved family members. Often a specific dish will come to mind, like your grandmother's famous apple strudel or your dad's smoked turkey.

Get started! Ask extended family to share cherished recipes and personal stories, such as who taught them to make the dishes. Then use the templates at Shutterfly (shutterfly.com/make-a-cookbook) and order your printed cookbook to enjoy for years to come. Or, buy an already-bound blank recipe book, such as *My Family Favorites Recipe Journal*, and fill it in by hand.

Cook Your Catch in Key West

After spending a day deep-sea fishing in the azure waters off Key West, Florida, sit back and relax while someone else prepares your "catch of the day."

Thanks to its access to the Atlantic Ocean as well as the crystal-clear waters of the Gulf Coast, Key West offers some of the best fishing in the United States. Knowledgeable captains will ferry you to the best locations to reel in sailfish, marlin, king mackerel, snapper, tarpon, barracuda, and tuna. These charter boats offer much more than just a ride. They provide the gear and expertise to guide even the first-time angler to a successful day on the sea.

On the ride back to town, you can enjoy the fresh salt air while they clean and fillet your fish so it's ready to be offloaded for dinner. Once you arrive back on land, the fish of your choice will be handed over to the restaurant to prepare for you. The remainder of your day's catch will be packaged on ice for you to take home.

Top off the perfect day with live music on Duval Street. Just wander around any night of the week and sample the different options. Don't forget to save room for the best Key lime pie, according to National Geographic and the Food Network, at Kermit's Key West Key Lime Shoppe.

Get started! Make your reservation at the Conch Republic Seafood Company, which will prepare your fish to order—blackened, lemon-peppered, or fried—while you bask in a stellar island sunset.

Enjoy a Japanese Tea Ceremony

On your visit to Kyoto, Japan, go beyond sightseeing and immerse yourself in a quintessential Japanese experience: a traditional tea ceremony. The point of the ceremony is to create a harmonious bond between the host and guest. As a result, every step is purposeful, beginning with your entrance to the traditional *chashitsu* tea house, where you'll bow low to pass through a small entryway, showing humility to gain access.

As you kneel in a posture called *seiza*, your host will prepare tea through a series of intricate steps. Although it may seem formal, don't feel intimidated. It is considered polite to be curious about your surroundings and ask questions. Mutual respect is paramount to the tradition, so you'll quickly learn to use the term *osakini* to other guests—this means "excuse me for going ahead of you"—before drinking your tea. Everything about the ceremony, from the layout of the room to the tea-making implements and process, is steeped in culture and history.

Participating in this ceremony in Kyoto, where the oldest and most acclaimed tea houses reside, makes the experience that much more special. Some tea houses even provide a traditional kimono for guests, whereas others allow you to join in modern clothing—though they do ask you to dress conservatively.

For other Japan experiences, check out page 27 and page 30.

Get started! To learn more about the tea as well as the ceremony, join the half-day Kyoto Uji Tea Town tour, where you'll visit tea shops, enjoy a luncheon of *cha soba* green tea noodles and other traditional dishes, and experience an authentic tea ceremony.

Indulge in Monastic Beer and Dumplings in Germany

Weltenburg Abbey, the world's oldest monastic brewery, is located on a bend of the Danube River in Bavaria, Germany. The Benedictine monastery was founded in the seventh century; the current baroque buildings were constructed in the early eighteenth century. It has passed between church and private hands over the years but was rededicated to the Catholic church in 1913. Today, you can tour the church dedicated to St. George and the brewery. Once you've enjoyed the interior, take a few minutes to walk around the grounds, which include outdoor stations of the cross.

The beer garden sits in the courtyard of the baroque-style monastery. Its claim to fame is the award-winning Kloster Barock Dunkel, a dark lager, the coloring of which comes from Munich malts. Brewed at the abbey in the traditional Bavarian style, the beer is stored in a rock cave until it is ready for you to enjoy. And if you're going to have a hearty German beer, there's nothing better than *semmelknödel* to go with it. Drenched in gravy, these hearty Bavarian bread dumplings are sure to fill you up.

Afterward, if you're staying in Kelheim, you can walk off your meal by returning on foot to burn off the calories. The 4.1-mile trail provides a final dramatic view of the abbey before wandering through the forest back to the city.

For another Germany adventure, see page 145.

Get started! The best way to experience the monastery on a beautiful day is to arrive by boat from Kelheim. You'll learn about the history of the area as you take in the dramatic sights of the Danube Gorge.

Forage for Fungi Italiano

Truffles are well known as a delicacy, and truffle hunting in Italy is an unparalleled gastronomic experience. Although there are more than 200 varieties of truffles, the crème de la crème is the white truffle—*Tuber magnatum pico*—of Alba, Italy. Valued at up to $4,000 a pound, they are affectionately known as white diamonds. Located in the Piedmont region of northwest Italy, Alba's surrounding oak forests create the perfect environment for the pricey fungus to flourish. Known as *tartufo* in Italian, this edible fungus is often confused with mushrooms. One primary distinction is that truffles grow underground, typically near tree roots.

Truffle hunting is so ubiquitous here that there is even a University of Truffle Dogs. Founded in 1880, the school trains dogs to sniff out the aromatic truffle and alert their master. A guided tour led by a regular truffle hunter, or *trifolao*, is the best way to experience this activity because each has their own secret spots that have been successful in the past. On the way to the location, you'll enjoy a great walk outdoors and learn more about the industry from a true insider, including truffle classification and hunting etiquette. Although you can't keep the truffles from your foraging adventure, many tours offer a cooking demonstration, lunch, and the opportunity to buy truffle-infused products.

Get started! White truffles can be found October through December. To make the most out of your trip, plan to attend the International Alba White Truffle Fair, held every weekend from mid-October to mid-November.

Experience Greek Gastronomy

Combine your love of history with unparalleled food by taking a culinary journey through Greece. Almost 13 percent of the total Greek labor force in the nation is employed in agriculture, which explains why so much of the region's food is based on fresh ingredients from small family farms. Cheese, grains, legumes, nuts, and olives play a central role in most dishes. With the longest coastline in the Mediterranean Basin, it's no surprise that fresh fish and seafood also abound in Greek food. Even better, much of Greece's hilly terrain is dotted with vineyards.

The country consists of the mainland and thousands of islands, 227 of which are inhabited. Specifically, there are nine geographic regions, and each has slightly different gastronomic traditions. Intrepid Travel is one of several operators that offers multiday guided gastronomic adventures. Its tour is based out of Athens and takes you to two islands (Aegina and Poros) as well as two villages on the Peloponnesian Peninsula.

Over nine days, you'll partake in fabulous food and activities. Highlights include a bike tour of the island of Aegina, where you'll visit a pistachio farm and try some delectable treats. You'll also participate in a cooking class on Poros, an island well known for its olive groves, and take a day trip to the car-free island of Hydra, where you'll enjoy a meal of spit-roast lamb.

Get started! Learn more about the tour and sign up at intrepidtravel.com/us/greece/greece-real-food-adventure-124485. Prepare for the trip by reading about the seven varietals of Greek wine at foodandwine.com.

Explore Swiss Alpine Cheesemaking

After you've ridden the rails (see page 26 and page 81), step back in time and experience the art of making cheese in the Alps. Switzerland might not produce the greatest volume of cheese, but it certainly makes some of the most popular varieties, like Appenzeller, Gruyère, and Raclette Suisse. A quick look at Alpine villages in any travel magazine will yield dozens of photos of cows wearing large bells wandering the steep mountainsides. The tradition of alpine cheesemaking harkens back to the Middle Ages, when the area was self-sufficient and dairy farming dominated the higher elevations. Making cheese became a common method to preserve milk. Alp cheese, or *Alpkäse*, is made with unpasteurized cow's milk and comes in semi-firm to firm varieties.

One of the best ways to learn about Swiss cheeses is to visit a Swiss show dairy. These dairies provide an opportunity to see how the cheese is made as well as sample a variety of flavors. Purchase some to take on a picnic during your Alpine walks. Much of the distinction in taste comes from the duration of aging as well as the cows' diet as they graze freely on the grasses and wildflowers in the mountains, so it is an essential part of the experience to walk the hillsides (or ride in cable cars) and see the cows roam.

Get started! Get prepared for your trip to the Alps by walking uphill as much as possible. To minimize pollution, most Alpine villages do not allow gas-powered vehicles. Although there are electric minibuses, most people get around by walking. Find a show dairy at cheeseconnoisseur.com/summertime-switzerland-adventures.

Learn North African Cooking in Marrakech

After your camel ride through the Sahara (page 25), if you're interested in learning more about North African cuisine, there's no better way than a cooking class in Marrakech, Morocco. Marrakech is home to a diverse range of influences, from French to Berber, and as a result, you'll find a wide variety of dishes to choose from. Because Marrakech is such a popular tourist destination, you'll be able to find cooking classes that cater to all levels of experience, from beginner to expert.

You'll typically begin with a guided trip to the local *souq* (market) where you can get guidance on choosing the best ingredients. Imagine winding your way through the bustling Jemaa el-Fnaa souq, the largest market in the country, sipping on delicious avocado juice (mixed with almond milk, it's more like a smoothie) as you feast your eyes upon the dizzying array of food, from dried fruit to braised camel.

Most Moroccan cooking classes feature the beloved local specialty known as tagine. Named after the domed dish it is cooked in, tagine is a spiced stew that features braised meat or fish and vegetables. It often contains sweet and savory flavors, like lamb with apricots and honey. Tagine isn't the only dish worth learning, though; pastry lovers will enjoy making dishes with *brik*, a paper-thin dough that is used in sweet and savory dishes alike.

Get started! Consider what type of cooking course you want to take, including duration of the lesson and number of menu items. Then browse the options on viator.com to choose the right one for you.

Perfect Wine Tasting in South Africa

If you've ever wanted to better understand the art of wine tasting, a sommelier course in South Africa is the perfect solution. Although there may be better-known wine regions, South Africa has the perfect climate for viticulture and has been producing wines from its idyllic vineyards since the seventeenth century. The pinotage red wine grape is the region's crown jewel, but South Africa is also notable in the industry for its sparkling wine produced using the traditional champagne method called *méthode cap classique* (MCC), where secondary fermentation takes place inside the bottle.

When you travel to South Africa, you can immerse yourself in the verdant wine regions of the Cape Peninsula. The Cape Wine Academy, located in the second-oldest wine region in the country, has been teaching wine enthusiasts since 1979. The academy offers wine sommelier certification as well as shorter courses for people who want to become connoisseurs of fine wines from South Africa and around the world. A great choice for wine enthusiasts who travel often is the one-day Wines of the World course. During guided wine-tasting sessions, you'll learn to taste and assess wines like an expert. With specific instruction on international grading systems, you'll be able to wow your friends and family with your detailed knowledge of wines. More important, you'll be able to confidently make the best pairings with food.

Get started! Read a book or take a quick online class to familiarize yourself with the basic sommelier terms. Order some South African wines from wine.com to prepare your palette.

Tantalize Your Taste Buds with Belgian Chocolate

For a decadent excursion that will delight your taste buds, tour the best chocolate factories in Belgium. Ever since chocolate was first introduced to Belgium by the Spanish in the seventeenth century, chocolatiers in the country have been working to perfect this delectable treat. The first innovation that put the Belgian chocolate game on the map was the creation of the praline. Swiss immigrant Jean Neuhaus Jr. used a mold to create chocolate shells and then added a soft cream or ganache filling. Today, you can still visit that original Neuhaus store in Brussels.

Belgian chocolate is known for its extremely smooth and creamy texture. If you've ever enjoyed chocolate produced in the United States, you will be astounded at the difference. Due to consumer laws, preservatives are added in the United States that make the chocolate more shelf-stable, but they can detract from that mouthwatering texture achieved by Belgian chocolatiers.

Chocolate factory tours in Brussels are so much more than a mere tasting. You'll start with a history lesson as you explore historical sites to learn how chocolate is a huge economic boon for the country and became iconic around the world. Once you arrive at the chocolate factory, you'll witness firsthand the transformation of the raw ingredients into the enticing treat we all know and love. Don't worry, you will get to sample a variety of tasty treats.

Get started! You have no shortage of chocolate tours to choose from on viator.com or getyourguide.com, but you'll have twice the fun by selecting a combination tour and chocolate-making workshop.

Dine on Ice in Finnish Lapland

At the Lainio snow village in Finnish Lapland, you'll find quite literally the coolest fine-dining experience you can have on earth. Each year, a winter wonderland is carved out of 40 million pounds of snow and 72,000 pounds of ice. The end result is a hotel, chapel, restaurant, and bar that create a unique structure each year. Elaborate ice and snow carvings decorate the walls, and multicolored light displays bring them to life.

In the restaurant and bar, the tables and chairs are carved from blocks of ice. But don't worry about sliding off (or freezing your backside), because you'll sit on strategically placed furs. Food in Lapland is often centered around reindeer and moose meat, so you'll find it roasted, smoked, and stewed in a number of dishes. Fish, such as salmon and arctic char in particular, is also an essential component of the local cuisine. You can find it baked into bread in a traditional dish called *kalakukko*. Other staples include root vegetables, such as fried Puikula potatoes and parsnip puree. Delicious cloudberry and lingonberry jams and confections top it all off.

After dinner, take time to tour the rest of the village. The ice chapel is particularly charming and often serves as a wedding venue. Finally, wrap up your visit with a stop at the ice bar, where you can enjoy lingonberry vodka and other liqueurs served in an ice glass.

For another Finland adventure, see page 85.

Get started! Dress warmly. As you might imagine, a giant ice structure is pretty cold . . . typically around 28 degrees Fahrenheit.

Savor Indigenous American Fare in Minnesota

It's impossible to fully recognize the significance of the Owamni restaurant in Minnesota without understanding the mission of Chef Sean Sherman. His goal is to reclaim Indigenous culinary traditions that were lost to forced assimilation during the nineteenth and twentieth centuries. The restaurant only serves what he calls precolonial food, including bison, rabbit, venison, and wild fowl. There is no farmed meat like chicken or beef or any processed foods like sugar or flour.

Taking their shared goal one step further, Sherman and co-owner Dana Thompson make every effort to source ingredients from tribal suppliers. Sherman is also the founder of the nonprofit Indigenous Food Lab, which aims to increase the number of those supplies. By sourcing bison from the Cheyenne River Reservation, he's supporting its efforts to restore the prairie and create an economic boost for the people who live there. To be true to these traditions, Owamni's menu is seasonal. The delectable bison tartare might be served with squash in one season and berries in another.

Situated on the shores of the Ḣaḣáwakpa (Mississippi River) in historic downtown Minneapolis, even the site of the restaurant has meaning. Named for Owámniyomni, it is a sacred site of peace to the Anishinaabe and Dakota peoples. *Owamni* in the Dakota language means "swirling water."

Get started! Peruse a copy of Sean Sherman's award-winning cookbook, *The Sioux Chef's Indigenous Kitchen*. More than a collection of recipes, it is a terrific primer of Indigenous foods in North America (sioux-chef.com).

Dine Mountainside in New Zealand

At just over 6,600 feet in elevation, the Pinnacles Restaurant, *Ngā Tohu* in Maori, is the highest dining establishment in New Zealand. It takes the phrase "dinner with a view" to a new level. Its fabulous lunch buffet is a great choice after morning hiking or skiing. The restaurant sits on Mount Ruapehu, one of three volcanos in Tongariro National Park. With floor-to-ceiling windows, it dazzles diners with sweeping views of the area. The park was deemed a UNESCO World Heritage site for its volcanic features and cultural significance to the Maori people. Keeping with the Indigenous culture, the menu features locally sourced dishes such as braised lamb from Waihi Pukawa farm.

Getting to the restaurant is an experience in itself. Take the Sky Waka gondola, which journeys up to the top of the mountain year-round. With only ten people per car, you'll have ample opportunity to enjoy the sweeping views on the one-mile ascent. On a clear day, you'll get a good look at the volcanic landscape with jagged peaks, deep valleys, and waterfalls.

Before your return down the mountain, you can hike the Whakapapa Skyline Walk to the ridge for an even better look at the Tongariro volcanic zone. It takes most people about an hour and a half to navigate the rocky terrain, but the payoff is worth it!

For another New Zealand adventure, see page 84.

Get started! Located in the center of North Island, this national park is not close to any major cities. Consider staying in the National Park Village to allow more time to explore.

Try Treetop Dining in Thailand

Get a bird's-eye view on fine dining by enjoying dinner in a bamboo pod hanging twenty feet up in one of Thailand's lush tropical rain forests. The upscale Soneva Kiri resort on the island of Koh Kood created this once-in-a-lifetime dining experience.

From the ground, up to four guests enter a pod made of locally sourced rattan and, once secure, are hoisted via cables to dining level in the trees. At this point, you might be wondering how the food arrives or, better yet, how to get a drink refill. Never fear, they have worked that out. Your meal and beverages are delivered by zip-lining waiters. The fare is casual but still meets the resort's high-quality standards. Adding to the whimsical feel of the entire experience, menu items like canapés in the canopy are appropriately named. Other offerings include galangal-spiced fish wrapped in banana leaves and organic salads made with fresh ingredients from the resort's garden.

Koh Kood is the least populated island off Thailand's coast, and as a result, unspoiled beauty abounds. This hidden gem offers quiet beaches, stunning waterfalls, and tranquil forest trails. Get to the island by speedboat or ferry. Once on the island, there is no public transportation, so you'll need to rent a motorbike or hire a *songthaew* (a modified truck used as a shared taxi) to get around.

Get started! Plan your visit for the right time of year. Westerners often plan vacations for the summer, but here you'd be in the midst of typhoon season. The best time to visit is between November and February.

Experience Hands-On Cooking in Hanoi

Markets are an exceptional way to learn about a culture's delicacies. In Hanoi, Vietnam, you can have your *bánh chuối hấp* (traditional Vietnamese cake) and eat it, too, by booking a combination market tour and cooking demonstration. The Dong Xuan Market, Hanoi's largest indoor market, sells a wide range of goods. The first floor is dedicated to food: local fruit, vegetables, seafood, and meat. To the Western tourist, the dizzying array of options and the art of haggling can be intimidating. That's where a guide will come in handy.

Typically, you'll meet your guide and travel to the market together, so you'll have time to discuss the menu in advance. That will help narrow things down at the market. Once you arrive, your guide will walk you through the stalls, providing instruction on how to select the best produce and meat. Next, you'll witness the art of the deal—the expected haggling that occurs before a price is agreed upon.

Once you've had plenty of time to enjoy the market experience, it's time to start cooking (and eating)! A popular dish to start with is pho, the traditional soup made with simmering beef broth, noodles, and fresh herbs. Next, you may learn to make *thit kho tau*, a classic comfort-food staple of caramelized pork belly. Top it all off with your bánh chuối hấp (cake!) for the road.

Get started! Travelingspoon.com is a terrific resource to find vetted local hosts to share their culinary traditions. Offerings include cooking demonstrations, homemade meals, and guided market visits.

Sample Street Food in Amman

If you love Middle Eastern fare, then a street tour in Amman, Jordan, is a gastronomic delight! *Fast, fresh,* and *delicious* are the common terms to describe the food you'll experience. Viator.com offers several half-day tours that typically begin with a walk around the historic sites of the city to give you time to work up an appetite in between food stalls.

The day will start with a *fuul*, a traditional breakfast dish made with fava beans, lemon juice, and chile. Enjoy it with coffee blended with cardamom seeds or tea steeped with sugar and fresh mint leaves. From there, you'll walk to Citadel Hill, or Jabal al-Qal'a, for the best views of the city. It connects to the Roman Amphitheater, which is one of the main tourist attractions. Moving on to Al Balad, you visit the bustling souks (markets), sampling fresh cane juice and snacking on nuts and dates as you peruse the wares.

No culinary tour would be complete without a visit to Rainbow Street, perched atop the hillside of Jabal Amman. This promenade of shops, cafés, and restaurants is aptly named for its colorful decorations. The most difficult part of the tour is trying to decide if you want to eat the falafel, *manakish* (flatbread topped with cheese and spices), or *kofte* (meatballs). If you're lucky enough to be traveling with family or friends, get them all and share!

Get started! Get a copy of *Recipes and Remembrances from an Eastern Mediterranean Kitchen.* Even if you never use the recipes, it provides valuable insight into the region's food culture.

Devour Pierogi and Polish Vodka

Like having a friend in a city, a good local guide is your best source of information. They always know the hidden secrets of a city and can steer you away from tourist traps—which is why there's no better way to fully immerse yourself in the authentic Polish experience than to share pierogi and vodka with a local guide.

Quick note on semantics: *Pierogi* is the plural form, and you won't need the singular (*pierog*) because you're going to want more than one! These delicious semicircular dumplings are stuffed with a wide range of savory and sweet fillings. Savory pierogi are filled with mushrooms and sauerkraut, fish, spinach, pork, potato, or a type of smoked cheese called *oscypek*. For dessert, try sweet cheese- and fruit-filled pierogi as well.

Once you've eaten your fill of delicious dumplings, you'll want to wash your meal down with a tasting of Polish vodkas. To earn the Polish vodka distinction, the liquor must be distilled from Polish-grown grains or potatoes. Wheat vodkas are considered smoother on the palette. Rye vodkas are found straight or flavored with a variety of berries, fruit, honey, and even hazelnuts. One unique flavored vodka is Żubrówka. It is flavored with bison grass from the Białowieża Forest—you can see a blade of the grass in the bottle. Finally, potato vodka typically has a milder taste than its grain-based counterparts.

Get started! Withlocals.com is a great website that provides experiences led by local residents. The site provides reviews so that you can learn more about each guide.

Drink a Dram in Scotland

A glass of heaven is awaiting you on the Malt Whisky Trail. While the abbeys in mainland Europe were making wine or beer, the monks of Scotland were getting creative with spirits. Their unique solution came in the form of malted barley mash. Initially dubbed *aqua vitae*, the water of life, whisky quickly became the quintessential beverage of Scotland.

There are more than a hundred Scotch whisky distilleries in this tiny country the size of South Carolina. Divided into five distinct regions—Campbeltown, Highland, Islay, Lowland, and Speyside—each has a unique flavor. Home to the Malt Whisky Trail, Speyside boasts more than half of the country's distilleries, which makes it a great place for you to tour.

The verdant valleys and fertile farmlands of northeastern Scotland make Speyside ideal for growing barley, the primary ingredient for its beloved beverage. Once it's harvested and combined with the sparkling clear water running down from the mountains, you end up with some of the best Scotch whisky the country has to offer.

The trail includes important historic sites and operational distilleries set among some of the most idyllic countryside you'll ever see. From rafting on the River Spey to trekking the peaks of Cairngorms National Park, there is plenty to keep you engaged throughout your visit. A trail highlight, in more ways than one, Dalwhinnie is the highest distillery in Scotland at 1,164 feet above sea level.

Get started! Rabbies.com offers some of the highest-rated Malt Whisky Trail tours. The three-day highlight tour provides a fabulous overview of both the natural wonders of the area and whisky distilleries.

Dine under the Outback Sky

Forget shrimp on the barbie—for an unforgettable Australian experience, dine under the stars at Uluru-Kata Tjuta National Park in the Australian Outback. The table is set at the base of Uluru, a massive monolith jutting into the sky. You'll sip champagne and eat smoked crocodile canapés as you enjoy the splendor of the setting sun.

The people at the Ayers Rock Resort created this iconic Sounds of Silence dining experience that honors the best features of the landscape. With minimal outside lighting, you'll dine on food sourced from Indigenous ingredients and enjoy Australian wines. Buffet offerings include Australian bush fare like barramundi and kangaroo. Once the sky is completely dark, a resident expert will share stories of the constellations.

Uluru is sacred to the Indigenous people of the region. You'll find ancient carvings and paintings in caves around the base of rock. Rising to a height of 2,831 feet above sea level, the world's largest monolith strikes a commanding pose in the desert. Its sandstone composition creates the orange color, which is especially dramatic at sunset. To set the stage for your evening and fully appreciate its connection to the Anangu culture, be sure to visit the Uluru-Kata Tjuta Cultural Centre earlier in the day. Once you've learned the creation story of Kuniya and Liru, walk about the site where a legendary battle from this myth was said to have taken place.

Get started! Because seating is limited, it is important to make reservations in advance. Go to ayersrockresort.com.au to save your seat and learn more about the other activities at the park.

Sip Madeira in an Island Paradise

What better way to sip on a unique style of wine than in its ancestral homeland? The verdant archipelago of Madeira is located 250 miles north of the Canary Islands in the Atlantic Ocean. It was discovered by fifteenth-century Portuguese explorers, and thanks to its fertile soil, vineyards were established not long after. Because of its high alcohol content and long shelf life, Madeira (the island's namesake wine) was often used as a bargaining chip during trading voyages. The heat and movement of the ships also helped improve the flavor of the wine, giving it a unique taste that is still prized today.

This delicious, fortified wine ranges from dry to sweet, making it a versatile choice for culinary pairings. Whereas most wines are sheltered from heat, warmth is actually crucial to producing Madeira wine. In fact, legend has it that the first Madeira wine was made accidentally when sailors left casks out in the sun. Smaller producers still heat and age it in the *canteiro* method by placing casks in attics to replicate the stuffy holds from those ships.

Blandy's Wine Lodge is in the capital city of Funchal and includes a museum as well as an active winery where you can see the entire process firsthand. You'll wrap up your tour with a tasting of the different varieties.

For another Portugal adventure, see page 83.

Get started! TAP Portugal offers direct flights from Lisbon and has a unique program where you can stop for an extended-day layover in Lisbon at no additional charge.

Picnic in Peru's Sacred Valley

Enjoy unrivaled scenery away from the crowds during a luxury picnic in the Sacred Valley of Peru. As it is the gateway to Machu Picchu, the region's most popular attraction, more than three million people flock to the Sacred Valley every year. That's why the solitude you'll find on this gastronomic excursion will be a welcome change of pace.

Known as the heartland of the Incan Empire, this fertile valley was key for maize production. Today, you can see the *andenes*, or agricultural terraces, they built on the hillsides to take advantage of varying levels of elevation to grow quinoa, root vegetables, and peppers. Beans, corn, potatoes, and other tubers are the four staples of many traditional Peruvian dishes.

Hosted by the Cicciolina restaurant in Cuzco, this destination luncheon truly is luxurious. Servers set up the dining area with linen tablecloths and ceramic place settings at one of four locations in the valley. The food is top-notch Andean fare, including ingredients that were grown in the surrounding farmland. There are menu options you can select from when you make the reservation, including roasted farm beet salad, yucca balls stuffed with Oaxaca cheese, quinoa-encrusted chicken, alpaca terrine, quinoa risotto with roasted farmer's vegetables, and so much more. You'll also enjoy the national drink, Pisco brandy, in the signature Pisco punch.

For another Peru adventure, see page 65.

Get started! The sacred valley sits at 8,000 feet elevation, and it's not uncommon for visitors to experience altitude sickness. Give yourself extra time to acclimate when you arrive.

Catch Norwegian King Crab

You're going to need to bring a big appetite on your King Crab Safari in northern Norway. About 250 miles north of the Arctic Circle is Kirkenes, Norway, a small town making a big name for itself in the red king crab market. You can visit year-round, haul in some of these tasty crustaceans, and feast on them shortly thereafter.

This is the same king crab found in Alaska. It was introduced to these waters in the 1960s and has now made its way to the deep fjords in the Barents Sea and has thrived there ever since. The king crab got its name for the pointed crown-like appearance of its barbed shell. These crabs are certainly big enough for a king's feast at up to twenty pounds!

Fishermen set crab pots in the fjord's seawater to catch them throughout the year. In the winter, your mode of transportation will be on a sledge pulled by a snowmobile, directly onto the frozen fjord. You'll join in as the fishermen break through the ice with an auger and pull the traps out of the water. In the summer, you'll go out in a rigid inflatable boat to pull the traps. Either way, once you've collected the day's bounty, you'll make haste to a warm hut so the crabs can be steamed, seasoned, and consumed.

For other Norway adventures, see page 72 and page 75.

Get started! The King Crab Safari is offered by the Kirkenes Snowhotel (snowhotelkirkenes.com/king-crab-safari) three miles outside Kirkenes. You don't need to be an overnight guest to book the excursion.

Trek the Kentucky Bourbon Trail

Enjoy bluegrass and southern hospitality as you sip your way across the state on the Kentucky Bourbon Trail. Due to its abundance of fresh limestone spring water and grain crops, Kentucky quickly became the bourbon capital of the world. It now produces 95 percent of the world's supply. A specific type of American whiskey, bourbon is distilled from a mash made primarily of corn and aged in charred oak barrels. The taste varies depending on the mash composition and age.

The Kentucky Bourbon Trail consists of forty-one distilleries across the state, each with its own distinct personality. Some have in-depth tours that walk you through the entire process from grain to liquid gold, whereas others are focused on the tasting room. Although you can travel the trail in any order, the official starting point is at the Frazier History Museum in Louisville. Even better, with four distilleries within a one-mile stretch, you can start your journey as soon as you leave the museum.

The Old Forester Distilling Company is a highlight, with four floors and an on-site cooperage where you can see the process of making the bourbon barrels. With many other attractions in Louisville, it is a great place to pace yourself and learn about the great state of Kentucky. Only an hour's drive away is Frankfort, where you can take a boat tour of four area distilleries.

For another Kentucky adventure, see page 61.

Get started! Several tour operators out of Louisville offer Bourbon Trail tours, so you can sit back and let someone else do the driving. They range from group tours in one city to multiday customized trips.

Join a Java Journey in Turkey

Coffee lovers will jump at the chance to learn the traditional art of making their favorite pick-me-up in Istanbul, Turkey. Turkish-style coffee didn't originate in Turkey, but it quickly took root there. The first coffeehouse of the Ottoman Empire was established in Istanbul in the sixteenth century. These Ottoman cafés were hubs of cultural and political activity. They brought together citizens from across all levels of society. Today, coffee still plays a major role in Turkish culture.

There really isn't a better activity in Istanbul to immerse yourself in local culture. Your coffee tour will start with a trip to a coffee shop for traditional Turkish sweets and a cup of coffee. Then you'll take a guided tour of the Spice Bazaar for coffee and cardamom. Finally, you'll make your way back to a café for the class.

Preparation of Turkish coffee is very precise and requires a specific grinder and pot. The coffee beans are ground to a very fine powder and mixed with water and sugar. Then the mixture is heated in a special pot, typically copper, called a *cezve*. Key to the Turkish coffee is the thick layer of foam on the top. It is important for that to be transferred to the cup, so your class will also include a primer on the perfect pouring technique.

For another Turkey adventure, see page 60.

Get started! Watch the documentary *Turkish Coffee Tales of Anatolia*. It aims to increase the awareness of the historical importance of Turkish coffee through stories of different coffee traditions that exist across Anatolia.

Give Molecular Gastronomy a Go

This exciting new culinary trend is gaining popularity by using science and uncommon cooking tools to create menu items that are both surprising and delicious. It is based on the premise that by understanding the molecular interactions that take place during cooking, we can create new and innovative dishes. Some of the techniques used in molecular gastronomy include sous vide cooking, spherification, and foaming.

The Fat Duck in Maidenhead, England, is one of the world's leading restaurants, and it is at the forefront of molecular gastronomy. Owner and pioneering chef Heston Blumenthal is known for mind-bending dishes that appear to defy gravity and traditional ingredients that have been transformed into something entirely new. For instance, consider one of Blumenthal's signature dishes: bacon and egg ice cream.

At the Fat Duck, Blumenthal adds whimsical and multisensory approaches to his dinner service. For example, he created a dish that included seafood foam on an edible beach. Calling it "Sounds of the Sea," he served it with an iPod so diners could hear the crashing waves while they enjoyed the dish. Don't worry if you're not sure what to try at the Fat Duck. It has a six-course tasting menu that includes signature dishes such as snail porridge and sous vide duck. And with its three Michelin stars, the restaurant is sure to delight and amaze your taste buds.

Get started! This restaurant is in demand, so make your reservations as soon as possible (thefatduck.co.uk). Then watch the BBC documentary series *In Search of Perfection* to understand Heston Blumenthal and his methods.

Feast at Maine's Lobster Festival

Attend the Maine Lobster Festival for five days of fresh lobster and fun! Lobster reigns supreme in Maine, and this festival celebrates everything about it. The food tent takes center stage with the tantalizing crustacean prepared in every way you can imagine and many you can't. The offerings start with classic boiled and buttered lobster plates and go from there to lobster bisque, lobster macaroni and cheese, lobster rolls, lobster-stuffed risotto balls, and lobster wontons.

Another gastronomic highlight of the week is the cooking contest. Amateur chefs from around the country compete for the top prize. The best part for you is that the audience gets to sample the dishes and get copies of the recipes. The dishes can be savory or sweet but must be made with Maine lobster and seafood. Previous winners have been lobster cheesesteak, lobster fried rice, lobster and seafood pasta, and lobster corn chowder.

Recognizing that great food needs to be accompanied by sensational spirits, the Steins & Vines tasting events showcase local beer and wines. Maine blueberry wine, mead, and cider provide the perfect refreshment on a hot summer day. There's more to do than eat, too: Every evening the festival hosts live entertainment. Musical acts include country, folk, jazz, rock and roll, and even an eighteen-piece Midcoast Maine–based big band.

Get started! See the full lineup of entertainment at mainelobster festival.com. While you wait for the festival, grab a copy of the book *The Lobstering Life* for a photographic journey of the men and women of Maine's lobster industry.

Nosh on Nova Scotia's Ocean Floor

For an unforgettable culinary adventure, dine on the ocean floor in the Canadian Maritimes. Nova Scotia's Burntcoat Head Park in the Bay of Fundy is home to the world's highest tide and most unique alfresco dining experience.

This activity is so much more than a great meal with spectacular scenery. Part education, part appreciation, it is a six-hour gastronomic journey. Your day begins with a lesson on local wild edible plants like dandelions, spruce, and wild carrots. Next, you'll be served a seafood luncheon on the bluff overlooking the bay. Enjoy the views from above before your post-lunch tour of the park.

By this point, the tide will be completely out, and you'll be treated to a walk on the ocean floor. As you're exploring the tidal pools and the high tide marks on the cliff above, the dining tables will be set for your three-course meal. You'll feast on locally sourced delicacies like grass-fed beef, lobster tail, organic vegetables, and seasonal fruit paired with local beer and wine.

If all that wasn't enough, you'll watch the tide start to come in from the comfort of an evening campfire. Save some time in your travel itinerary to go back in the morning and see the bay during high tide. Imagine your dining room covered in fifty feet of water!

Get started! This special meal is only served six to eight times each summer. The dates for each season are released early in the year (January or February). Look for them at foodfantastique.ca.

CHAPTER THREE

EMBRACE NEW EXPERIENCES

For many of us, retirement is the first time in our lives when we have the opportunity to pursue interests we have only dreamed about. In this chapter, I hope to inspire you to try new experiences and reach for the stars. Think about your hobbies and interests and consider where you could really indulge them. If you love kayaking, maybe you'll want to try it with orcas. Always wanted to learn to ballroom dance? Learn the tango in Argentina. Whatever you choose to do, retirement is a time to enjoy life and make the most of your newfound freedom.

Fly over Ancient Turkish Caves

Soar in a hot-air balloon over the unique rock formations in Cappadocia, Turkey. Known as fairy chimneys, these dramatic natural features dot the countryside, and they reach up to 130 feet high. Imagine floating over them as the sunrise changes the color of the rocky terrain. You'll ascend into the morning sky either right before or after sunrise and may reach an altitude of 3,000 feet. Your pilot will raise and lower the balloon so that you can get a bird's-eye view of the spectacular scenery. Coupled with more than a hundred hot-air balloons, it's a sight you won't soon forget.

Get started! Cappadocia is a region in Turkey with several towns you can select among for your visit. Göreme is a great choice with plenty of hotels and balloon-tour operators. Learn more at hotairballooncappadocia.com.

Live Like a Local Abroad

If you are an animal lover, house-sitting is one of the best ways to visit a foreign country. You'll get to stay in someone's home for free in exchange for caring for their pets. You'll live like a local and save money on your travels. Because the pet owners have a vested interest in making it an enjoyable experience for everyone, they will often introduce you to neighbors or provide insider tips to highlights of the local area, like favorite restaurants and markets. You can find both short- and long-term requests from just one week to a few months or longer.

Get started! Join trustedhousesitters.com to set up a profile and browse requests from vetted homeowners around the world. Start with a short stay close to home, and then build from there.

63

Race to the Checkered Flag

Experience the power and precision of a Formula 1 race car as you speed around some of Europe's most iconic tracks. Feel the g-forces as you take tight corners and fly down straights at top speed—it's an adrenaline rush like no other. LRS Formula offers experiences that range from two hours to six hours, including a briefing on how to operate the car, training in a pilot car, and laps in the single-seat race car. You can race on one of five different tracks in France, Portugal, or Spain, each with its own unique challenges.

Get started! Go to lrs-formula.com/en to learn more about the different cars and tracks available for this exciting adventure. If you'd prefer not to drive, you can also choose a modified three-seat race car and ride as a passenger.

64

Explore the World's Largest Cave System

After you've had your bourbon fix (page 53), go spelunking in Mammoth Cave National Park in central Kentucky and see what adventures await. Home to the world's longest cave system, it's the perfect place for cave explorers of all levels, with more than 200 caves to explore, there's something for everyone. You never know what you might find around the next corner—a new passage, an underground river, or even a waterfall! For a unique activity, take a stroll through the historic caves by lantern light. If you're more daring, try an introduction to caving that will lead you through tight spaces into smaller chambers.

Get started! To explore the cave system, you will have to join one of the tours led by the National Park Service staff. (nps.gov/maca)

Swing at the "End of the World"

For a high-flying thrill, the Swing at the End of the World at La Casa del Arbol in Ecuador is the perfect place for you! The original tree house, or Casa del Arbol, was built as a monitoring station for the nearby Tungurahua volcano, but today there is a swing attached (with a harness) that allows you to soar over the Ecuadorian wilderness. This iconic attraction has been featured in movies, TV shows, and travel blogs all over the world. It's no wonder why—with a view like this, it's hard to resist.

Get started! You have four options to get to Casa del Arbol: a bus that leaves from the town center, a taxi, a tour company, or, if you're feeling adventurous, a hike.

Experience the "Mistery" of Niagara Falls

Nestled between New York State and the Canadian province of Ontario, Niagara Falls is truly a sight to behold. Standing at the edge of the falls, it's hard to believe that water can flow with such force. It's even more amazing to ride on the *Maid of the Mist* boat and feel the power of the falls firsthand. During this unforgettable twenty-minute boat tour, you'll pass the American Falls as you head toward the main event, Horseshoe Falls. As you near the base, you'll feel the power of 600,000 gallons of water per second crashing down around you. It's an incredible feeling that will leave you breathless.

Get started! Tours leave every fifteen minutes, so you won't need a reservation. They include a complimentary rain poncho. Trust me, you're going to need it!

Raft through the Grand Canyon

Carved over the course of millions of years by the Colorado River, the Grand Canyon is one of the most iconic natural wonders in the world. And there's no better way to experience its majesty than by rafting through it. These guided adventures will have you braving white-water rapids and floating through idyllic canyons. Options include a three-and-a-half-day trip through part of the canyon and a full two weeks for the whole 225-mile journey.

If the idea of rowing that long makes you tired, don't worry. The guides do all the work. The reason most river tour operators also have motorized rafts is to allow you to complete the same distance in a shorter amount of time. Regardless of which tour you choose, a typical day on the river includes learning about the history and geology of the area from your guides, enjoying breaks on the sand banks, and even taking short side hikes to vantage points. You'll stop in the late afternoon, allowing plenty of time to set up camp, eat a hearty meal, and socialize around a campfire. Each night, you'll sleep under the stars and be amazed at how different life looks far away from the hustle and bustle of daily life.

Many of the trips end with a hike to the rim of the Grand Canyon. From the rim, 4,000 feet above the river, you'll be amazed when you look down at the distance.

Get started! Grand Canyon Whitewater (grandcanyonwhitewater .com) offers several different Grand Canyon rafting tours. Take the short quiz on the website to determine which one is best for you.

Go "Flight-Seeing" over Hawaii

You've probably seen pictures of Hawaii's rugged and majestic shorelines—now imagine viewing them from above! A helicopter tour is the best way to take in all the natural beauty Hawaii has to offer. From the moment you take off, you'll be mesmerized by the incredible scenery that unfolds before you, from active volcanoes and gorgeous waterfalls to lush rain forests and pristine beaches. And since a helicopter can reach places cars and buses can't, you'll be able to see parts of the island most visitors never get to experience.

Sprawling over 4,000 square miles, the Big Island of Hawaii is a diverse island, brimming with natural beauty. There is so much to see that it's hard to experience it all without a little help. The tour company Blue Hawaiian Helicopters' Big Island Spectacular was voted the world's best helicopter thrill by Travel Channel. Its two-hour narrated tour gives you a bird's-eye view of Kilauea, one of the planet's most active volcanoes.

From the volcanic badlands, you'll fly over black sand beaches and some of the most spectacular waterfalls with cascades over a thousand feet. Add on the Laupahoehoe Nui landing and you'll get up close and personal with a 1,200-foot cascade and have time on the ground for about twenty minutes of exploration before taking to the air for a view of the Kohala Forest Reserve on your way back.

Get started! Fly early in your trip to get an overview of the island and scout out places you'd like to visit on the ground.

Sleep on the Side of a Peruvian Cliff

Imagine you're having a really great dream in which you're snoozing among the stars on a peaceful mountainside—only you wake up and it's real. That's what you can experience when you stay at Skylodge Adventure Suites. Here, you'll sleep in a glass room 1,200 feet up a mountainside, overlooking the valley and surrounded by stars.

Reaching Skylodge is an adventure in itself. With a professional guide, you'll hike and climb up the mountain using a *via ferrata*, a system of anchors, cables, and ladders. Your guide doubles as a chef, and once you reach your pod, you'll be rewarded with a gourmet dinner prepared while you take in the breathtaking view of Peru's Sacred Valley. Looking out, you'll see a winding river, farmland, and jagged mountain peaks.

The capsules themselves are twenty-four feet wide and have four beds, a private bathroom, and an area for dining and simply enjoying the view. Don't worry, they aren't really made of glass, it just looks like it—instead, they are constructed out of aerospace aluminum and weather-resistant polycarbonate. After a night under the stars, you'll wake to the sunrise over some of the most spectacular scenery you've ever seen in your life. Breakfast is served alfresco on a platform atop the pod. Then you'll be in for another thrilling treat as you descend using a series of zip lines.

For a different Peru adventure, see page 51.

Get started! The journey up to your hanging hotel room is physically demanding. Be sure to give yourself time to acclimate to the altitude of the Peruvian Andes before your stay.

Do the Tango in Argentina

Tango is more than just a dance—it's an experience that will transport you to another world. The sensuous choreography is often called an embrace, due to the connection of the dancers. If you've ever wanted to learn how, there's no better spot than its birthplace, Buenos Aires. Here, you'll learn from the best and dance in the heart of this vibrant city. Join a multiday tango tour to get a complete immersion into the dance and the city that gave birth to it.

You'll start with a dinner and dance show, providing an introduction to the world of the Argentine tango. The next day starts with a tango shoe shopping excursion to get you outfitted for your lessons. Between dance classes and practice sessions, you'll tour the city and surrounding area including the Plaza de Mayo, Casa Rosada (the president's residence), and the Colón Theater.

Evenings allow time to visit tango clubs, which are a great place to practice and revel in the local joy for this iconic dance. Even better, all that dancing works up an appetite for the culinary delights of Buenos Aires. Dine on perfectly grilled steaks with chimichurri and pastries stuffed with creamy dulce de leche, all while enjoying a glass of the area's world-renowned wine. The architecture, history, and culture all come together to create an unforgettable experience—one you can only have by learning to tango in Buenos Aires.

Get started! Argentinatango.com offers packages ranging from a three-day weekend experience to a two-week tango holiday. Choose the one that is right for you.

Snowshoe in the Canadian Rockies

Snowshoeing is one of the most popular ways to experience the Canadian Rockies in all their chilly glory. Banff National Park, the largest park in the Canadian Rockies, is one of the most beautiful places on earth, and in the winter, it's a wonderland of snow-covered trees and frozen lakes. For a winter activity that will take you into the heart of nature, consider experiencing it on foot in snowshoes.

The Lake Louise Ski Resort offers several snowshoeing options from snowshoe rentals for self-guided adventures to lessons and guided tours. A great introduction to this activity and the Lake Louise summit area is the scenic snowshoe tour. An expert will provide instruction on how to use snowshoes and then lead you on a one-and-a-half-hour journey around the Ptarmigan Ridge while regaling you with stories of the geology and history of Lake Louise. Your guide will also help you identify the various wildlife tracks you're sure to find in the snow. Your tour also includes a ride back down to the resort on a scenic gondola. In addition to viewing the majestic beauty of Victoria Glacier, many visitors are rewarded with sights of wildlife seen grazing under the gondola's path.

Wrap up a day on the trails by soaking your muscles in the naturally heated water of Banff's Upper Hot Springs.

For another Canada adventure, see page 80.

Get started! The farther away you get from the towns and ski lodges, the more likely you are to encounter wildlife. If that's on your bucket list, look for one of the longer snowshoeing tours.

Sleep under the Stars

There's nothing quite like lying down under the night sky and admiring the stars. But due to all the artificial light we rely on, most people can't see the Milky Way at night. That's why finding an out-of-the-way spot, far from human habitation, is so important. You will be amazed at how close and bright the stars appear when you visit an area without light pollution. It's a humbling experience that illustrates just how tiny you are in the vastness of the universe.

The Greater Big Bend International Dark Sky Reserve in southwest Texas is the largest of twenty dark sky reserves in the world. The International Dark Sky Association awards this designation based on the exceptional quality of starry nights. The reserve covers more than nine million acres of the Chihuahuan Desert, including Big Bend National Park and Big Bend Ranch State Park. Its remote location (288 miles southeast of the nearest big city) creates the perfect conditions for celestial viewing.

The two parks join forces to present night sky programs to ensure you get the most out of your experience. These programs are run by expert astronomers who will help you find and identify different constellations you can see with the naked eye and through their telescopes. They also share stories about the history and mythology of the night sky.

Get started! Nestled between Big Bend National Park and Big Bend Ranch State Park, the villas and cabins of Lajitas Golf Resort in Lajitas, Texas, provide a perfect base for your visit.

Giddyup on a Cattle Ranch

Carving a living from the land is the stuff of legends, and there's no better way to experience it than at a working ranch. You'll get to know the sights and sounds of the early pioneers who started herding cattle on this land—but in a bit more comfort.

TX Ranch, home to almost 1,000 head of cattle and 100 horses, straddles Montana and Wyoming between the Bighorn Canyon National Recreation Area and the Pryor Mountains—and it also hosts visitors. There's nothing quite like horseback riding across the plains, feeling the wind in your face and the sun on your back. You don't need to be a seasoned rider, either. The ranch staff will select your horse and assign you to a team based on your personal experience. Guests can choose their level of activity as well. You are invited, but not required, to participate in all the ranching chores, including mending fences, baling hay, and irrigating pastures.

From sleeping in cow camps at night to driving cattle during the day, you'll have the experience of a lifetime. After a day's work, you'll enjoy hearty home-cooked meals served in a log cabin, followed by an evening around a campfire. Accommodations include canvas-walled tents with comfortable cots and separate bathhouses. It's a great opportunity to learn about a different way of life and to get in touch with your inner cowboy.

Get started! Vacation packages at TX Ranch (txranch.com) include six full days of riding, cattle drives, and seasonal ranch activities. To understand the changing landscape of the west, read *The Last Cowboys: A Pioneer Family in the New West*.

Try Your Hand at Falconry

Raptors have been used in hunting for thousands of years, and you can get firsthand experience in this historical sport by taking a class in the United Kingdom. Falconry is the ancient art of training birds of prey to hunt and to follow their human counterpart. You will start by learning about the different species, essential equipment, and how to care for the birds before progressing to flying and hunting exercises.

The Hawk Conservancy Trust in Andover has numerous courses, ranging from one for a complete beginner with no knowledge of falconry to an advanced professional certification program. The trust is a twenty-two-acre nature reserve that is home to more than 130 species of birds of prey, including owls, eagles, and kites.

The first step in falconry is getting to know various raptors, and the conservancy has the perfect course to help you learn all about them. During its full-day Bird of Prey Experience, you'll be introduced to many birds, and their trainers will guide you through every step of the process, from handling your bird for the first time to flying them through the skies. Typically, you'll have the opportunity to fly an eagle, hawk, and owl. If you'd like a multiday course, consider the acclaimed Beginning Falconry Award Course offered through a partnership with Amews Falconry. The four-day course spends a significant amount of time on husbandry in addition to flying.

Get started! If you're not sure about taking the longer falconry certification course, you can visit the conservancy to see the birds, watch demonstrations, or participate in a two-hour orientation.

Swim with Sharks in the Maldives

Being in the water with these magnificent creatures may seem like a scary prospect, but it is actually an exhilarating experience. There's no better place to do it than the crystal-clear water of the Maldives, a series of islands in the Indian Ocean. With about 1,350 square miles of reef, it abounds with marine diversity. There are more than twenty different species of sharks in the area, including hammerhead sharks, nurse sharks, reef sharks, and the massive whale sharks.

One of the most unforgettable experiences is swimming alongside a whale shark. At eighteen to thirty-three feet long, whale sharks are the world's largest fish. Although the thought of swimming with these predators may be daunting, it is actually very safe. These massive creatures are truly gentle giants called filter feeders—no huge sharp teeth. The best place to see these magnificent sharks is the South Ari Marine Protected Area at the southern end of the atoll, where you'll have the opportunity to observe these amazing creatures up close and personal.

The LUX South Ari Atoll Resort is a perfect base for your adventure. Located in the protected area on the small private island of Dhidhoofinolhu, guests can choose from bungalows on the beach or villas on stilts over the water. The resort offers guided snorkeling and diving excursions around the area to find the best spots to see the marine wildlife.

Get started! Whale sightings are common year-round in the South Ari Atoll. For drier weather and calmer seas, plan your trip from November to March.

Mush Huskies in Norway

Dogsledding is the perfect way to experience the stunning landscapes of northern Norway. Nestled between mountains and fjords, this part of the country is a popular destination for outdoor enthusiasts, and there's no better way to explore it than by dogsled. Numerous dog-sledding tours operate out of the cities of Tromsø and Alta. Typical half-day excursions are led by experienced guides who will teach you the basics of mushing, take you for a ride on a sled, and even let you try your hand at driving the team.

Even better are the more intensive multiday expeditions in which you will drive your own team of dogs through pristine forests, along towering mountains, and across frozen lakes for up to five hours a day. Your guide will point out features of the tranquil countryside and help you spot wildlife. As a member of the team, you'll also care for the dogs along the way.

In the evenings, you'll dine on traditional fare like *bidos* (reindeer and vegetable stew), *fiskesuppe* (fish soup), and *multekrem* (cloud-berry cream dessert). Accommodations on the trip include a modified lavvo (a traditional Sami tent) with a wood-burning stove to keep you warm. The lavvo also has floor-to-ceiling windows so you can fall asleep under the stars or, if you're lucky, the northern lights.

For other Norway adventures, see page 52 and page 75.

Get started! Because snow is required, the best time to travel for dogsledding is January through April. If you have to travel later in the year, you can still go on a kennel tour and interact with the dogs.

Splurge on an Overwater Bungalow

Imagine waking up to the sound of waves splashing below you. The sun is just peeking over the horizon, and the water is a beautiful turquoise. You step out onto your private deck and jump into the cool water for a morning swim. This could be your reality if you splurge on an overwater bungalow in Bora-Bora. Don't worry—*bungalow* doesn't mean "tiny." In fact, with a separate living room, bedroom, and bathroom, each bungalow is larger than some apartments. Each one has its own deck, and many also have their own pools.

Bora-Bora, a French Polynesian island located about 230 miles northwest of Tahiti, is an idyllic island destination, renowned for its clear waters and pristine beaches. Since it is surrounded by a lagoon and a reef, water sports are a prime activity. You can go snorkeling right from your porch in the morning and then take an afternoon nap in a hammock.

If you can tear yourself away from your bungalow for a few hours, the island features Mount Otemanu and Mount Pahia—both beautiful spots for a jeep tour or a hike. Yes, that's right, there is more to Bora-Bora than the beach. Whether you're looking for a relaxing beach vacation or an action-packed adventure, Bora-Bora has something for you.

Get started! With so many options, choosing the best resort is the hardest part. The Le Méridien has the largest glass floor panels and great views of Mount Otemanu from across its private lagoon.

Find the Far Side of the Moon

Witness a spectacular celestial phenomenon by experiencing a total eclipse. In a total eclipse, the disk of the sun is fully obscured by the moon. This can only happen when the sun, moon, and earth are perfectly aligned. For anyone within the path of totality, it's an amazing event. The sky darkens and the temperature drops as the sun's light is completely blocked out. Stars and planets become visible, and the corona—the outermost atmosphere of the sun—shimmers in the darkness. Totality lasts for just a couple of minutes, but it's an unforgettable experience. If you're lucky enough to find yourself within the path of totality, don't miss your chance to see a total eclipse.

Since the moon is smaller than the earth and sun, it casts a relatively small shadow. You have to be in the center of that shadow to witness the eclipse, which is why a total eclipse can only be seen from certain parts of the planet when it occurs. If you wait for one to find you, it may not happen for about 375 years for the pattern to repeat a similar path. That means if you want to witness an eclipse in person, you'll have to go in search of it. NASA's solar eclipse website (solarsystem.nasa.gov/eclipses) projects the occurrences through 2030 and identifies them by type.

Get started! Cloud cover will impact your experience, so try to pick a place in the path of totality that will have better weather. Be flexible and keep an eye on forecasts.

Cruise through Fantastic Fjords

Carved out by glaciers, Norwegian fjords offer some of the most stunning and dramatic landscapes in the world. One of the best ways to explore this natural wonder is by electric boat, which allows you to access the narrow inlets' nooks and crannies. The boats' wide decks offer panoramic views of the towering peaks, deep valleys, and pristine waterways you'll experience on your journey.

The country boasts more than a thousand fjords, but only two are on the UNESCO World Heritage List: Geirangerfjord and Nærøyfjord. Among the world's longest and deepest, their unparalleled beauty comes from the steep rock walls that rise up over 5,000 feet above sea level. Your breath will be taken away at every turn by sites covered in deciduous trees and stunning waterfalls.

Combine your boat tours with the famed Flåm Railway on the acclaimed Norway in a Nutshell tour. Over twelve miles, you'll descend 2,800 feet through the scenic Flåm valley, where you'll disembark for your cruise, a two-hour tour along the Sognefjord, Norway's deepest fjord. Spend a day exploring Bergen, Norway's second-largest city, before embarking on a full-day cruise to the beautiful Geirangerfjord tour. Along the way, you'll see some of the most famous waterfalls, including the Bridal Veil and Seven Sisters. The latter is named for its seven streams, the tallest of which falls more than 800 feet into the fjord.

For other Norway adventures, see page 52 and page 72.

Get started! Find the tour at norwaynutshell.com to customize your trip. Although it can be done in two days, experts recommend you spend some time exploring the small villages in the fjords as well.

Celebrate at a Powwow

By immersing ourselves in other cultures, we can learn about each other and become more accepting of our differences. Attending a powwow is a great way to learn about Indigenous cultures in the United States. Powwows are events that recognize Indigenous history, honor Indigenous ancestors, and are celebrations with family, food, and friends. Because each tribal community has its own traditions, powwows can vary in different geographical areas.

However, some things are very common across all powwows. For instance, the circle is central to a powwow. In most cases, the dancers are at the center with drums forming a larger circle around them. Competitive dancing and music are important ways for Indigenous Peoples to share traditions that were once prohibited in the United States. Typically, several different types of dances are performed at the powwow, each with its own regalia. The powwow begins with what is known as the Grand Entry, where all the dancers enter in a line. All attendees should stand during the Grand Entry. There will also be times when everyone will be invited to dance if they choose. Feel free to admire the endurance of this tradition and even join in respectfully when invited.

In addition to music and dance, you can expect to see beautiful handmade crafts, hear traditional stories, and taste delicious Indigenous American cuisine.

Get started! Some powwows are private, but most are open to the public. Find a powwow near you and learn more about appropriate etiquette by reading the frequently asked questions at powwows.com/main/native-american-pow-wow.

Commemorate Mongolia's Independence

The annual Naadam Festival in Mongolia, held in July, is a lively multiday event that dates back to the twelfth century but now celebrates Mongolia's independence from China. It's a unique festival with food, dance, and elaborate costumes that showcase local traditions, but the primary focus is on three specific types of competitions: archery, horseback riding, and wrestling. Known as the "games of men," the contests originally were aimed at showcasing military prowess. However, women can now compete in all events except wrestling.

You'll marvel at the prowess of the contestants in the three different archery styles, each with their own unique bows, arrows, and targets. Men, women, and children showcase their marksmanship over two days. During the wrestling portion, 512 contestants compete to be the last man standing under these basic rules: touch the ground with any part of your body except arms or feet and you're out. A fascinating part of this event is the *zasuul*, or encourager, who sings the winning wrestler's praises. The final event is the horse race. It's not held on a track like Western horse racing—it's a long-distance, cross-country race in varying distances. Due to Mongolia's nomadic roots, horses are integral to the traditional Mongolian way of life, and children learn to ride young. Riders in the Naadam competitions are typically children ages seven to thirteen.

Get started! The main Naadam festival takes place in the country's capital Ulaanbaatar, drawing huge crowds. Since Naadam is a national festival, you can find local Naadam celebrations in most towns and villages.

Scale the Namibian Sand Dunes

Sossusvlei in the Namib Desert is one of the most incredible, otherworldly places on earth. You will feel small next to the gigantic sand dunes. Depending on the sunlight, the colors of the dunes range from pink to burnt orange and every hue in between. The contrast between them and the clear blue sky is something to behold.

Big Daddy is the highest dune in Namib-Naukluft National Park. It is massive, towering 1,000 feet above the desert floor. You can hike up the dune, but be prepared for a lot of work, and carry more water than you think you'll need. If you can start before or just at sunrise, you'll have an easier time of it. Once you reach the top, you'll be astounded by the amazing views of the surrounding desert and the other dunes.

If climbing Big Daddy seems too much of a feat, there are alternatives. Dune 45 (named for its distance in kilometers from the entrance) is very impressive at 550 feet. Coincidentally, it takes most visitors about forty-five minutes to an hour to climb to the top. Finally, Elim Dune at 300 feet in height is wonderful and much less crowded.

Get started! Stay at the Sossus Dune or Dead Valley Lodges inside the park to avoid long entry lines. They allow access to the dunes at sunrise, before the park opens to other visitors. The park is pretty remote, but you can take a multiday tour from Windhoek, the capital of Namibia, or even Cape Town, South Africa.

Trek Majestic Kilimanjaro

Standing at a staggering 19,341 feet tall, this majestic mountain is one of the most popular hiking destinations on the planet. Aside from Mount Kilimanjaro's iconic status as Africa's tallest mountain, another draw for hikers is that the hike isn't technical—meaning you won't need special mountaineering gear or skills. In addition, hikers can take several routes to the top, which decreases crowding on the trails.

One of the oldest, the Marangu route, has huts (think dormitories and dining halls) rather than campsites along the way. A great one-day option for you is to take a guided trek to the first hut, Mandara, where you can walk to the rim of Maundi Crater and see the stunning views of Mawenzi and Kibo Peaks in the distance. You'll start your journey by going through the rain forest at the base of the mountain, gaining almost 1,500 feet in elevation as you hike up the mountain. It doesn't sound like much until you consider that you're starting at more than 7,500 feet above sea level. This means that unless you live at high altitude, you'll need time to acclimate yourself. The best way to accomplish this is to arrive in Arusha a few days early. There are plenty of day trips and activities to enjoy while you adjust.

Get started! You can trek up Kilimanjaro any time of year, but it is much more enjoyable during the drier months of June and October. If you don't mind colder weather, January through March is the least crowded alternative.

Get Up Close and Personal with Polar Bears

The Hudson Bay area of Manitoba, Canada, offers an experience like no other . . . the chance to see the world's largest concentration of polar bears. Each fall, Natural Habitat Adventures offers lucky visitors the chance for a close encounter (but not too close!) with these magnificent creatures.

Specially designed vehicles called polar rovers will transport you and fifteen other wildlife enthusiasts to the Churchill Wildlife Management Area, where the polar bears often congregate waiting for Hudson Bay to freeze so they can start their winter hunting season on the ice. The bears are drawn to this particular bay because its freshwater freezes earlier than saltier spots, giving them first dibs at the hunting grounds. This trip provides three days and one evening out on the tundra to maximize your chance of polar bear encounters.

The rovers aren't a typical tour bus. They were made for your comfort and safety. Every passenger has a large window seat and the option to walk out on the rear viewing platform when the vehicle is not in motion. It's high enough off the ground that the seven- to nine-foot-tall giants can't reach you and also includes corrugated steel-mesh flooring so you can see any bears that are below it.

As a special treat, upgrade your accommodation to the Tundra Lodge, a rolling hotel the company moves around high-bear-density areas. Another upgrade is a helicopter tour to spot other wildlife like caribou and moose.

For a different Canada adventure, head to page 67.

Get started! If this trip is on your bucket list, don't delay! As ice season shrinks, the polar bear population is declining. Book your trip at nathab.com/polar-bear-tours.

Step Aboard the World's Steepest Rail

Stoosbahn is more than just a transportation system—it's an adrenaline rush! With a gradient of up to 110 percent, or 47 degrees, the world's steepest funicular connects the Swiss town of Schwyz to the tiny alpine village of Stoos.

The Stoosbahn is a funicular rail, which means it's a dual cable rail with the two cars balancing each other. As one ascends the mountain, the other descends. You'll journey up the mountain on this unique track, gaining 2,441 feet over 1.1 miles as you enjoy views of the French Alps. It has another unique feature: barrel-shaped carriages that rotate as the rail rises up the mountain to maintain a level floor surface for its riders.

Once out of the tram, take a deep breath of the fresh mountain air, made fresher by the lack of cars. The only ways to get to Stoos are via the funicular or on foot. Speaking of your feet, let them do some walking on one of the many trails. An easy crowd-pleaser is the Stoos Ridge Hike with views of magnificent Lake Lucerne and several mountain peaks. The short version is only three miles by taking one chairlift up, walking the 2.7-mile Ridge trail, and then going back down to the village on another chairlift. For a longer version, you can skip the chairlifts and make it an 8.2-mile loop.

For other Switzerland adventures, see page 26 and page 37.

Get started! Stoos is located thirty-seven miles south of Zurich. You can reach it by car or via the train to Schwyz and the 501 bus to the funicular.

Kayak with Killer Whales

Washington's San Juan Islands are home to many wonders, but for many thrill seekers, the orcas take top billing. Growing up to thirty-two feet long, these majestic creatures are some of the largest predators on the planet, and being able to see them up close is an unforgettable experience.

Given that orcas are known as "killer" whales, many people wonder if it is safe to get so close to them in the wild. By joining a guided tour, you'll learn everything you need for a safe adventure and have a trained professional looking out for you.

Get started! The best time to kayak with orcas is from late spring to early fall. Sea Quest offers tours ranging from a half day to five days to maximize your time with the orcas.

Go for Gold in the Yukon

For hundreds of years, people have traveled to the northernmost reaches of North America in search of gold. Imagine the experience of standing in an icy cold mountain stream (with waders!), surrounded by the beauty of the Yukon wilderness while panning gold.

Gold was first discovered in the Yukon in 1896, and it wasn't long before prospectors from all over the world rushed to the region in search of their fortunes. They faced many challenges and much of the territory is still wild today. The dreams of finding gold in the Yukon continue to hold a special place in adventure seekers' hearts.

Get started! Dawson Creek is the best place for visitors to learn more about the Klondike gold rush. Start with a tour of historical sites and then try your hand panning for gold at Free Claim 6.

Dare to Traverse the World's Longest Foot Bridge

The 516 Arouca suspension bridge in Portugal is one of the most unique and breathtaking bridges in the world. Suspended 570 feet over the Paiva River Valley, the bridge spans 1,693 feet and offers breathtaking views of the surrounding mountains and forests. Made of metal, the floor is a grid that allows you to see the valley and gorge down below—all you have to do is ignore that voice in your head that says "don't look down." Since this is a suspension bridge that hangs from reinforced girders, be prepared for some movement as you walk, particularly if other people are on the bridge with you.

The bridge is located in the Arouca Geopark, which is recognized by UNESCO for its unique geology. There is so much to do here, you could easily spend an entire day or more. The park also has a 5.5-mile series of raised wooden walkways that descend in a zigzag pattern over 500 steps down to the Paiva River. At the base, there are beaches for swimming as well as areas for kayaking and rafting.

Encompassing 127 square miles, the park offers fourteen hiking trails featuring waterfalls, caves, and overall fabulous views. The nice thing about many of these trails is that they not only meander through the natural features and identify important geological formations, but they also go through several small villages.

To pair your trek with a Portuguese wine excursion, see page 50.

Get started! Only an hour's drive from the city of Porto, the Arouca area is a great day-trip destination. If you'd like to visit as part of a guided tour, visit getyourguide.com.

Cruise in a Campervan around New Zealand

New Zealand is a land of contrast: snow-capped mountains and pristine beaches, thermal hot springs and bubbling mud pools, glaciers and subtropical forests—all within close proximity. The best way to see as much as possible is to rent a campervan (a small van-style RV) and explore at your own pace, stopping to camp overnight in some of the most scenic spots in the world.

If you've never been to New Zealand, you can see the highlights of both the North and South islands in a two-week tour from Auckland to Christchurch. You'll drive 650 to 850 miles depending on the route you take. That includes a ferry between the two islands.

The great thing about seeing the country this way is that you can stop whenever you want and have your lodging and transportation in one. When you rent, be sure that you choose a self-contained campervan, meaning it has a small kitchen, freshwater tank, and toilet. You'll be able to take showers at campgrounds, called holiday parks, along the way. For those who want to get off the beaten track, there are also primitive campsites in natural areas managed by the Department of Conservation. Finally, many remote sites on public land, where you can truly appreciate the natural beauty of New Zealand, allow overnight parking.

For another New Zealand adventure, see page 43.

Get started! Motorhome Republic (motorhomerepublic.com) is a third-party booking service that will allow you to compare a wide selection of RVs. It also has a wealth of information about the process and driving in New Zealand.

Ogle the Northern Lights from an Igloo

Deep in the heart of Finnish Lapland, on the edge of the Arctic Circle, sits the Arctic SnowHotel & Glass Igloos. This unique destination is the perfect place to experience the colorful display of the aurora borealis. As night falls, you can cozy up inside your igloo and watch as the sky lights up with a dazzling display of colors.

The specially designed igloos were made for comfort. With heated glass roofs and underfloor heating, you'll be perfectly comfortable on even the coldest of nights, with the added advantage of keeping ice from obstructing your view. The beds are motorized to allow you to adjust them for the best possible viewing position. Finally, you don't have to worry about falling asleep and missing the precious sight of the northern lights: The igloos come equipped with alarms that notify you when they're visible.

The Arctic SnowHotel has several unique features, including a snow sauna. Believe it or not, you can sit in a hot steaming sauna with walls constructed of ice and snow without them melting around you.

Before you settle in for an evening in your igloo, you can feast on roast elk or braised arctic ocean salmon in the hotel's restaurant, which is carved out of ice. Finish off a perfect night at the ice bar, where the drinks are as cool as the scenery.

For another Finland adventure, see page 41.

Get started! Reservations for the glass igloos are available every year from late September to mid-March. Learn more about the resort and book your stay at arcticsnowhotel.fi.

CHAPTER FOUR

GIVE BACK

There are many reasons why you should consider volunteering in your community or abroad. For one, helping others can simply be gratifying and satisfying. Knowing that you are making a difference in the lives of others can be a huge source of joy and purpose in retirement. Volunteering is also a great way to stay socially engaged. By volunteering, you'll connect with other people who share your interests. Finally, it can be a great way to stay mentally sharp and physically active. Studies have shown that volunteering can help reduce the risk of cognitive decline and memory problems.

Hatch and Release Sea Turtles

Nestled in a lush jungle along the coast of Costa Rica, the Pacuare Reserve is home to a variety of wildlife, including the endangered leatherback sea turtle. On a critical nesting beach, volunteers play a vital role in the success of these turtles. During nesting season (March through May), you and other volunteers walk the 3.7-mile beach and help collect eggs and build protective enclosures for the hatchlings. Once the turtles have hatched (June through September), you'll release them into the sea and monitor their progress. Throughout the year, the reserve also offers educational tours of the area showcasing other conservation efforts.

Get started! The Pacuare Reserve can create a custom volunteer plan for you, including a stay in a cabin at the Casa Grande Eco Lodge. Learn more at pacuarereserve.org/volunteer.

Garden for the Greater Good

For many people around the world, gardening isn't a hobby—it's a way to ensure a steady supply of nutritious food. Every year, billions of people are affected by food insecurity, and gardening is a terrific solution to this problem. That's why Global Volunteers offers gardening programs in countries all over the world. They will train you to build and plant garden boxes, and in turn, you'll help the local community use them to grow their own food. In just a few weeks, volunteers can make a lasting difference in the lives of those they work with, helping ensure a more food-secure future for everyone.

Get started! Global Volunteers has gardening programs in Cuba, Peru, St. Lucia, and Tanzania. See the options at globalvolunteers.org.

Lace Up to Cure Cancer

Participating in a walkathon is a great opportunity to come together with your community to support a worthy cause. The American Cancer Society Relay For Life raises vital funds to support their life-saving mission to prevent and treat cancer. Join a team or form your own; camp out at a local park, school, or fairground during the relay and take turns walking around a track or pathway for twenty-four hours. Events are held overnight to represent the fact that cancer never sleeps. It is typically a community event with food trucks and local musicians to keep the motivation going.

Get Started! Each year, more than 5,000 walkathons are held in communities across the United States and thirty countries around the world. Find one near you at acsevents.org.

Help Save the Rain Forest

If you'd like to help the planet by combating climate change, then a trip to Brazil should be high on your list. The Iracambi Rainforest Research Center is working to reverse the trend of deforestation in the Atlantic Forest along Brazil's eastern coast (it has lost more than 80 percent of its original tree cover) with the help of volunteers like you. You'll work together with the local volunteers to help farmers prepare their land for new trees in addition to many other tasks, like water sampling, nursery work, planting, and monitoring new tree growth.

Get started! The Iracambi Rainforest Research Center's flagship program, Forests4Water, has already planted more than 160,000 seedlings. Visit iracambi.com/projects/forests-4-water to plan your trip and help reach its goal of one million trees.

Nurture a National Park

Many people dream of spending extended periods of time in national parks, but many parks restrict stays to no more than two weeks. However, the National Park Service offers a volunteer program that provides lodging in many of the national parks for free in exchange for twenty-four hours of work per week for three to six months. Lodging ranges from cabins to small dormitory-style rooms and even some RV campsites with water, sewer, and power. Parks typically make every effort to ensure couples work the same hours so that they can enjoy their time off together.

There are many different types of positions to choose from, so you are guaranteed to find something that interests you. Even better, for the vast majority, no experience is required. One of the most common positions is campground host, where you'll check in campers and do light maintenance. Other positions include gate attendant, visitor center desk, or even administrative support. If spending time out-doors is more to your liking, there are volunteer jobs for back country patrol, invasive species eradication teams, and trail guides.

Finally, there are volunteer positions based on specific skills. For example, Cedar Breaks National Monument in Utah and Curecanti National Recreation Area in Colorado are always looking for people with astronomy knowledge to help with their educational programs. And California's Lassen Volcanic National Park has an artist in residence program.

Get started! Browse for opportunities at volunteer.gov. You can search by date, difficulty, location, or specific volunteer position. The dates required and time commitment are clearly defined.

Uncover the Past

If you love history, then an archaeology expedition might be the perfect summer adventure for you. Archaeology is the study of human history and culture through the examination of artifacts and other remains—and you can be a part of it. Just imagine sifting through the dirt to reveal a pot or arrowhead that's been buried for centuries. It's an amazing feeling, knowing that you are the first person to lay eyes on something that's been hidden away for so long. And it's not just about the thrill of the find. Archaeologists learn a lot about the people who created these artifacts, how they lived, and what they believed in.

As a volunteer, you'll learn about the process of excavating and cataloging historical artifacts. You'll work alongside professional archaeologists contributing to important research projects that could shed new light on long-forgotten civilizations.

One particular area of ongoing research that requires volunteers is in the Tagus Valley in Portugal. For years, researchers have investigated the valley in search of clues about the Mesolithic–Neolithic transition, a dramatic shift from hunting or gathering to farming culture. By helping uncover important artifacts, you'll make a direct impact on historians' understanding of this evolution of humanity. On the expedition, you'll spend your days exploring ancient ruins and piecing together the puzzle of the past.

Get started! Earthwatch has been leading archaeological expeditions since 1975, when it began excavation of mammoth sites in South Dakota. Find the perfect opportunity to get involved at earthwatch.org.

Farm for Our Future

If you love farm-fresh food, take the opportunity to get your hands dirty (no, really dirty) by working on a farm. World Wide Opportunities on Organic Farms (WWOOF) connects volunteers with organic farmers and helps promote sustainable agriculture practices. Formed in the United Kingdom in 1971, the group offers opportunities in more than a hundred countries.

Depending on the type of farm you choose, you will help with a variety of tasks, from planting and harvesting to caring for farm animals and making compost. Are you handy with tools? Every type of farm always needs maintenance and repairs. Volunteers typically work four to six hours per day in exchange for room and board, and they have the opportunity to learn about organic farming methods while getting a taste of rural life.

Lodging can range from a private room in the host family's home to a separate cabin. Locations include small family-run farms, orchards, ranches, and vineyards. Examples include an olive orchard in Cyprus, a small organic vegetable farm on the coast of Argentina, an avocado and citrus orchard in the United States, a botanical garden in Slovenia, and a sheep farm in northern Finland. The length of stay is often negotiable, from two weeks to a few months.

If you've ever wanted to learn something new, work outside, and experience a different culture, consider giving WWOOFing a try.

Get started! Information about the program can be found on the WWOOF website (wwoof.net), but to search for farm stays, you'll need to select a country and purchase an annual membership.

Save the Strays

If you love animals but don't want the long-term commitment of adopting a pet, then fostering is a great option. Every year, millions of cats and dogs are brought to shelters in the United States. Although some of these animals are eventually reunited with their families or adopted into new ones, others are not so lucky. Each year, around 2.7 million cats and dogs are euthanized in shelters due to a lack of homes. This is a tragedy that can be prevented, at least in part, by foster care programs.

When people foster animals, they provide a temporary home for them until they can be adopted. This not only helps reduce the number of animals in shelters, but it also allows the animals to thrive in a home environment. Dogs and cats are social creatures that benefit greatly from being part of a family. Fostering provides them with this opportunity and gives them a better chance of being adopted into a permanent home.

If you have the available time for more intensive support, many animals need assistance after surgery or other medical procedures. Of course, there are always puppies and kittens that need a little extra tender loving care. If you love animals and have room in your home, consider fostering an animal in need.

Get started! Your local animal shelter is a great resource for fostering opportunities. The shelters will typically conduct a home visit, provide an orientation, and ask you to sign a contract outlining responsibilities.

Share Your Language Skills

There are many reasons why you might choose to teach English as a second language, both at home and abroad. For many people, teaching English is a way to fulfill their desire to help others. It can also be a great way to meet new people and learn about their cultures as well. And for those who want to travel, teaching English provides an opportunity to see the world while making connections with people who live in different places. In both cases, the organization hosting the program will provide you with the tools and training you need to be successful.

If you're interested in teaching English as a second language, first, you'll have to decide where. Teaching English at home can be a great way to help recent immigrants thrive—just think about the challenges of communicating with their children's teachers, making friends in their neighborhood, and even preparing for citizenship exams without knowing the language. You can help!

Teaching abroad often focuses on teaching English to children in schools or conversational English to adults in community settings. Global Volunteers is an international organization that hosts programs in twelve different countries in Africa, Asia, Europe, and South America. Trek to Teach is a unique program that takes volunteers to remote villages in the Himalayas (on foot) to teach English in primary schools for twelve-week sessions.

Get started! If you want to volunteer in your community, check for programs with your local library. To volunteer abroad, look at a reputable organization like Global Volunteers (globalvolunteers.org).

Make Peace around the World

You might think that the Peace Corps is only for recent college graduates, but hundreds of volunteers over age fifty are serving around the globe. Although the program is open to people of all ages, your wealth of experience and knowledge can be particularly valuable contributions. Another reason mature adults are well suited to this service is that you also tend to be highly adaptable, which can be a valuable asset in unfamiliar and challenging environments. Finally, older adults in the communities you serve may be more open to working with someone closer to their age.

Volunteers serve as individuals or as a couple for a two-year term in one of the following areas: agriculture, community economic development, education, health, or youth development. You may find yourself promoting health and wellness in Ecuador, facilitating sustainable agriculture in Jamaica, coaching budding entrepreneurs in the Dominican Republic, supporting water sanitation efforts in Peru, or teaching secondary school in Sierra Leone.

The great thing about the Peace Corps is that you apply for a specific position, so you choose where you'll be placed and what you'll be doing. The listing will include any specific requirements, including education, experience, or language skills. You'll live within the community you serve, making friendships that will last a lifetime.

Get started! Most positions require a bachelor's degree, but there are some that accept five years of relevant experience. Some also require specific language skills, but most do not. See current volunteer needs at peacecorps.gov/volunteer/volunteer-openings.

Rescue the Coral Reefs

The coral reefs of the Florida Keys are some of the most beautiful and biodiverse ecosystems in the world. But these fragile ecosystems are under threat from climate change, pollution, and overfishing. The good news is that there is something you can do to help. The Coral Restoration Foundation is the world's largest coral reef restoration organization, and it is always looking for volunteers. By getting involved with their efforts, you can play an active role in protecting and restoring coral reefs.

Whether you are a certified scuba diver or want to help on land, there are opportunities for you. One of the ways you can help is by participating in the foundation's coral nursery program. Located in Key Largo, the nursery is home to more than 35,000 coral fragments. They are grown by volunteers and then transplanted onto coral reefs. The nursery also serves as a research facility, working to develop new methods of coral propagation. Divers assist with the planting on the reefs as well as monitoring the existing coral transplants.

Volunteer programs require a minimum three-week commitment. If you're unable to visit the Florida Keys for that long, you can also participate in the two-day immersive diving program. Participants receive a lecture on the foundation's work, get a hands-on tour of the nursery, and go out on charter dives to learn how to identify signs of coral reef decline in nature.

Get started! The Coral Restoration Foundation was founded to combat the loss of coral reefs in Florida. Learn more about the volunteer opportunities at coralrestoration.org/volunteering.

Beautify Your Beach

Each September, the Ocean Conservancy organizes a worldwide event called the International Coastal Cleanup with volunteers like you. On a single day, people all over the world head to their local beaches to pick up trash and debris. This annual event makes a huge difference in the health of our oceans and shores. You can get involved by organizing a beach cleanup in your local area.

This effort is crucial to keeping trash from ending up in the ocean every year, where it hurts wildlife, damages habitats, and threatens human health. Some types of marine debris, such as plastic bags and Styrofoam, can take years to break down. Most of this trash comes from land-based sources, such as littering and improper waste disposal. Once it enters the water, it can be carried long distances by ocean currents. This means that even if you live far from the coast, your actions can still have an impact on the health of the ocean. So, as you can see, beach cleanup is a significant tool in improving the health of our waterways.

The Ocean Conservancy makes it easy by providing all the materials you need to get started, including a detailed planning guide, trash data cards, and tips for engaging your community. Trash data cards are used to track the types and quantities of trash collected, which helps inform future cleanups. The Ocean Conservancy also offers an app for documenting and mapping trash on beaches, to assist with important research efforts.

Get started! Learn how to organize your community to join the International Coastal Cleanup this year at oceanconservancy.org.

Scout Scenic Rivers for Science

If you love spending time outdoors and are interested in helping protect our nation's waterways, then you might want to consider volunteering with Adventure Scientists. It is a nonprofit organization that partners with government agencies like the Bureau of Land Management, National Park Service, and U.S. Forest Service to survey water quality in protected rivers across the country. It is always looking for volunteer canoeists, kayakers, and rafters because they can reach even the most remote river systems.

The quality of our water is essential to both our environment and our health. Ten percent of the drinking water in the United States comes from our rivers. Unfortunately, polluted rivers are all too common, and their negative effects can be felt for miles downstream. That's why Adventure Scientists volunteers survey water quality in these natural sources nationwide. By collecting data on everything from pH levels to the presence of microplastics, they help identify areas of concern so that scientists can develop strategies for improvement.

Adventure Scientists will provide all the training you need via online recordings and live webinars with Q&A sessions. It also ships field probes and other collection equipment to you prior to your project start and reimburses you for shipping samples back to its lab. It's a great partnership to match outdoor enthusiasts with researchers to help protect our waters for generations to come.

Get started! To see a map of the rivers included in the project and find out more about how you can become a citizen scientist today, visit adventurescientists.org/rivers.

Scuba with Whales

Take the chance to support conservation efforts for an endangered species. Due to overfishing and pollution, whale sharks are now an endangered species. In fact, their total population has dwindled by almost 50 percent over the past seventy-five years. All Out Africa's Marine Research & Whale Shark Conservation project gives volunteers the opportunity to help protect these incredible animals. The project is based in Tofo, Mozambique, a fishing village on the Ponta da Barra peninsula along the Indian Ocean.

You'll receive training to help scientists with whale shark research and data collection. You might even get the chance to tag and release juvenile sharks back into the wild. Whale sharks are filter feeders who flock to this area when the plankton blooms between October and March. Each day, you'll head out to sea to snorkel alongside the whales, taking photos and making observations on their behavior, size, and any other distinguishing features. On other days, your research activities will focus on the reefs, marine plants, and other fish. Their health affects whale sharks as their food source.

If you are unable to go during those dates, there are many other marine projects occurring at the institute throughout the year. During the months of June through October, volunteers climb sand dunes and go out on boats to spot pods of migrating humpback whales.

Get started! Programs last from two to twelve weeks. If you plan to join for fewer than four weeks, you'll need your scuba diving certification. For the longer stays, you'll earn it there.

Bring History to Life

Make history more accessible by volunteering at a living history museum, a type of museum that focuses on re-creating historical settings and periods. Visitors to a living history museum can expect to see buildings, furnishings, and clothing from a particular time period. These museums offer interactive activities, such as demonstrations, workshops, and hands-on learning opportunities.

As a volunteer, you will dress in authentic period costumes and play a role illustrating what daily life was like during the era you are representing. The largest living history museum in the United States is Colonial Williamsburg in Virginia. Here, visitors experience life in the eighteenth century by talking to townsfolk who share what daily life was like from the perspective of different trades. Walk into the apothecary to hear what medical remedies were used, or visit the blacksmith's shop to learn how they made everything from horseshoes to pots and pans.

The nation's first living history museum is Greenfield Village in Michigan, where visitors can explore more than eighty acres of historic sites, including a one-room schoolhouse, a working farm, and a general store. It is laid out in seven districts with the highlight featuring Henry Ford's contributions to the automotive industry. The Railroad Junction district chronicles the history of rail transportation in America.

Get started! Due to the training involved, there are typically specific commitments required of volunteers. At Colonial Williamsburg, volunteers work at least ten hours per week for a year.

Bring the Biodiversity

Get involved in local conservation efforts by identifying flora and fauna in your community. Even better, get your friends and family involved by planning a community BioBlitz. National Geographic Society's BioBlitz is an event that encourages people to get outside and explore the natural world. The goal is to document as many local plants and animals as possible in a short amount of time (typically a single day or a weekend), helping to create a snapshot of local biodiversity.

You can make your event as simple or elaborate as you want. You can ask people to just record everything they see or focus on specific plants and animals that are known to be in the local area. The easiest way to record observations is to use iNaturalist, a National Geographic app that identifies plants, animals, and even insects with a smartphone. The great thing is that the app also tells you if the plants you see are native or non-native. If you want to offer a no-tech option to participants, you can print out worksheets.

The data collected can be used to help protect and preserve local ecosystems. In addition, the event helps raise awareness of the importance of conservation and stewardship. National Geographic's BioBlitz is a fun and rewarding way to learn about the natural world and what we can do to protect it.

Get started! Download the free guide to BioBlitz at national geographic.org/projects/bioblitz. It offers plenty of ideas for recruiting partners, local naturalists, and volunteers to help make your event a success.

Adopt a Trail

Hiking and nature trails are popular recreation spots for good reason. They offer a chance to get away from the hustle and bustle of everyday life, enjoy some fresh air and scenery, and get some exercise. However, without proper care, trails can quickly become overgrown and littered. That's why adopting a trail is such a great idea. By taking on responsibility for maintaining a section of trail, you can help keep it clean and clear for everyone to enjoy.

Adopting a trail is typically a quarterly commitment, and your duties will include clearing the trail of debris, maintaining the trail markers, and reporting any hazardous conditions. Hand tools are often supplied, as power tools are not usually authorized in wilderness area. Sometimes the park will ask trail maintainers to band together for larger projects. In exchange, you may receive perks such as free parking and access to special events.

If you don't feel comfortable maintaining a trail on your own, you have two options: You can organize a group of friends to be on your trail crew, or you can join an existing one. Many local hiking clubs adopt trails as a group and send two or three people out together. Then those smaller groups alternate so that they can care for the trails monthly rather than quarterly. The regular upkeep makes it easier to stay on top of any problem areas.

Get started! Local, state, and national parks are always looking for volunteers to adopt a trail. Contact a park near you to learn about its needs.

Lead the Charge for Charity

When it comes to giving back, there are many different ways to do it. You can volunteer your time, donate goods, or raise money for charity. Although all options are important and effective, fundraising allows you to support an organization's work toward a cause you really care about. When you raise money for charity, you pool resources from many different people and have a greater impact than you could if you gave on your own.

There are many different types of fundraisers you can hold, from charity auctions and fun runs to more elaborate events such as gala dinners. One very simple way to support a good cause is to host a bake sale for Cookies for Kids' Cancer, a national nonprofit that funds innovative therapies used to treat childhood cancer. Get creative and make it a fun community event with a cookie-decorating contest, or pair it with a national bone marrow registry drive.

Work with local partners to increase your event's success. Seek out local businesses to sponsor your event to increase your revenue. You might even be able to recruit your local radio station to show up, which will increase publicity. The organization will also help you set up an online donation page you can share with people who are unable to attend the day of the event but would like to contribute.

Get started! The most important thing is to choose a cause you really care about. Once you do that, find an organization that the money will go to and coordinate with it on the fundraiser.

Be a Soldier's Home for the Holidays

The holidays can be a tough time for military personnel who are away from home. They often spend the holidays on base, far from their family and friends. One way to show your appreciation for the men and women who serve our country is to invite a soldier to join you for a holiday meal. Whether it's Thanksgiving, Christmas, or any other special occasion, sharing a meal is a great way to show your support for those who sacrifice so much. It's also an opportunity to learn more about the men and women who make up our Armed Forces.

This is also such a simple way to give back—all you need to do is offer a seat at your table. If you're interested in hosting someone for a holiday meal, keep a few things in mind. First, check with your local military base to see if there are any guidelines or restrictions in place. Next, be sure to plan ahead so that you can accommodate any dietary restrictions or allergies. Most important, be yourself. Share your traditions and listen to theirs.

This simple act of kindness not only provides a warm meal and a sense of community for a service member who may be away from home, but it also helps build bridges between civilian and military life.

Get started! Operation We Are Here (operationwearehere.com) maintains a list of organizations that match airmen, sailors, and soldiers with people like you who want to host them for the holidays.

Blanket Kids with Love

Being in the hospital can be very scary for anyone—and even more so for a child. It can also be isolating when they are cooped up and away from their friends. One way to brighten their day is to make them a blanket. This simple gesture can bring some warmth and comfort to a child during their stay. You don't even have to know how to sew. Fleece no-sew "knot" blankets are treasured by children.

Fleece & Thank You is an organization that supplies colorful fleece blankets to hospitals in thirteen different states. You can purchase a kit directly from the organization, and it will include all the supplies you need to make a sick child's day. Even better: You can organize a group to participate in a blanket-making event! Fleece & Thank You provides a guide to help you organize an online or in-person project with templates and video tutorials.

In addition to the blankets, it asks that you provide a short video message. This often ends up being the highlight of the gift. According to the organization, the children love seeing who made their blanket and hearing their words of encouragement. Once your blankets are made, you can send them to Fleece & Thank You, or you can volunteer to join one of its blanket delivery teams.

Get started! Fleece & Thank You (fleeceandthankyou.org) has all the information you need to plan your blanket-making event. If you don't feel crafty yourself, you can also purchase blanket-making kits for others.

Protect the Pollinators

Learn about bees and explore Costa Rica while helping protect some of the world's food source! Sounds like a tall order, but Earthwatch makes it easy with its pollinator program.

Over three-quarters of the world's plants and crops rely on pollination from bees, birds, bats, and other animals. Costa Rica alone has more than 400 species of wild bees, many of which are in danger of disappearing due to habitat loss and pesticide use. Their decline has been linked to a reduction in the abundance of certain fruits and vegetables. Earthwatch is working to protect these crucial pollinators through a variety of educational programs, habitat restoration projects, and research initiatives. You can help by joining one of its trips to Costa Rica, where you will have the opportunity to assist with field research, learn about local pollinators, and take part in habit restoration efforts.

Volunteers have the opportunity to work with local farmers and beekeepers to learn about beekeeping practices and help with hive maintenance. They also work with local schoolchildren, teaching them about the importance of bees and other pollinators. Another critical task is planting "agroforests" to benefit pollinators. The organization coordinates with local communities, which has the added benefit of providing sources of income for them. By helping conserve wild bees, you'll play an important role in protecting the environment.

Get started! Earthwatch's efforts in Costa Rica are focused on education and outreach as well as on hands-on conservation projects. Find a project that is suited to your interests at earthwatch.org.

Study Rhinos in the Wild

The rhinoceros is one of the world's most iconic species, but it is also one of the most threatened. There are only five species of rhino left in the world, and all are at risk of extinction. African rhinos are particularly vulnerable, as they are being poached for their horns at an alarming rate. By joining a conservation expedition, you can help protect this amazing species and ensure that future generations will be able to enjoy them.

Earthwatch is a leading environmental organization that is working to conserve threatened rhinos in Africa. As part of this effort, its researchers are studying the impact of rhinos on their environment. What they learn is essential for developing effective conservation strategies.

On your twelve-day expedition to northwest South Africa, you'll start with orientation and two days of training to ensure you understand the methodology and equipment. Then you'll head out to the field to see these majestic creatures and observe their behavior, making note of their location and group composition, feeding habits, and other interactions. You'll also make note of other mammals and birds, both in places where you find rhinos and in places where none are spotted. This helps researchers better understand the interactions between other animals and rhinos. If you have ever wanted to get up close and personal with African wildlife, this is the perfect opportunity for you.

Get started! This is an ongoing research project requiring volunteers year-round for a wide range of activities. Learn more about this important project and how you can help at earthwatch.org.

Deliver Food and Friendship

Homebound adults are one of the most vulnerable populations when it comes to getting enough nutrition. They may not have the ability to cook for themselves, or they may not have family or friends nearby who can check in on them. That's where you come in. Meals on Wheels is a program that delivers nutritious meals to their homes, and it relies on volunteers to help with meal delivery. Volunteers typically work in teams of two, and they use their own vehicles to deliver the meals. Deliveries are typically made once a week, and each route takes about two hours to complete.

But food is just one part of what you're providing to your homebound neighbors. You're also providing much-needed social interaction, showing them that they aren't alone. Almost one in four homebound seniors lives alone. They may not see one other person during the week, so they look forward to your stop. Just remembering their names and taking a few moments to share a conversation goes a long way toward boosting a homebound adult's emotional health.

As a volunteer, you are also the eyes and ears of the organization. You may notice changes in a recipient's health or mental status before anyone else. By reporting this back to your local organization, you can ensure that they get the help they need quickly.

Get started! There are more than 5,000 local Meals on Wheels community programs in the United States combatting hunger and senior isolation. Find one near you at mealsonwheelsamerica.org.

Build the Future

Many people struggle to find a place to call home. They may live in substandard housing or even experience homelessness. Habitat for Humanity is an organization that helps address this problem by building affordable homes for families in need. Volunteers play a vital role in this process, as they provide the labor required to construct the homes. No matter what your experience or skill set, there is a role for you to play in the construction of a Habitat home.

Even if you have never picked up a hammer before, you are welcome. All you need is a willingness to learn, and you will be trained on a wide variety of tasks. Habitat will always have experienced personnel on-site to provide training and assistance throughout the day. You also won't be asked to do anything that you don't feel comfortable doing. It truly is a team effort.

You can volunteer in your local community or travel to a build site. Habitat's Care-A-Vanners program offers a unique opportunity for RV owners to support home-building efforts at a specified location that also provides space at a nearby campground. You can also travel internationally with its Global Village short-term service trips to build homes around the world. By donating your time and effort, you can help provide a family with a safe and affordable place to call home.

Get started! Whether you are looking for a local volunteer effort or a travel opportunity, find the best project for your needs and schedule at habitat.org/volunteer.

Commune on a Reservation

In the 1800s, the American government forced Indigenous Peoples onto reservations to make way for colonization of their ancestral homelands. Reservations were often located in remote areas with little access to vital resources like water and timber. In addition, the government placed strict limits on what Indigenous Peoples could do with their land, making it difficult for them to sustain themselves economically. There are still lingering problems associated with these awful policies. In addition to supporting policy changes through political activism, you can also get involved and volunteer to support an Indian reservation.

Global Volunteers is an international organization that provides volunteer opportunities at the Rosebud Indian Reservation in South Dakota and Blackfeet Indian Reservation in Montana. Working closely with tribal leaders, it supports projects that are specifically requested and ensures that all volunteer efforts are culturally sensitive. Each summer, it offers several one- to two-week-long projects supporting the following areas: home repair and maintenance, food assistance, children's summer activities, and elder care.

During the day, you'll volunteer your services working alongside community members, providing you the chance to form a bond with others. In the evening, you'll enjoy group dinners and learn more about the tribal community you're supporting. You'll also have the option to participate in cultural events like powwows or individual ceremonies. For instance, many volunteer teams are invited to attend a traditional sweat lodge ceremony on the Blackfeet reservation.

Get started! Visit globalvolunteers.org to choose from one of several summer sessions at the two reservations.

Support Nepalis in Need

Nepal is a country of great natural beauty, but it faces many challenges. Now you can indulge your love of travel and experience the country's majestic landscapes while helping those in need. Nearly half the country's population lives below the poverty line, and it has one of the highest rates of child mortality in the world. ChildFund International and Global Volunteers work in partnership to provide support for community development efforts in Nepal. Their goal is to help build a foundation for long-term change by providing essential resources and training opportunities for Nepali children and families.

Volunteers work with local partner organizations to provide needs-based support in areas such as education, economic development, and health care. Education is key to developing long-term opportunities. If you are interested in this area, you may provide assistance in the classroom or through after-school tutoring. For those who have computer or other vocational skills, Global Volunteers partners with Soroptimist Kathmandu, a local nongovernmental organization providing employment training for women. If you'd rather work with your hands, there are plenty of opportunities to build or restore existing infrastructure. Healthcare professionals are always in demand to help provide preventive health care and education.

On the weekends, local partners accompany volunteers on sightseeing excursions, allowing you to experience the country's natural assets and cultural history. Highlights include a tour of Kathmandu, a visit to the medieval village of Bhaktapur, and a sightseeing flight over Mount Everest.

Get started! The program is run from February through November of each year, allowing volunteers several dates from which to choose. Explore the options at globalvolunteers.org/nepal.

Tour Your Town

If you love your city and enjoy meeting new people, you might consider offering local walking tours. You'll be providing a great way for visitors to see a city from a different perspective while you share tidbits about the area's history and culture. If you're interested in becoming a tour guide, follow a few steps to get started.

First, develop a theme around your interests. Whether you are highlighting architecture, history, or even haunted places, a theme will keep you focused and your guests engaged. Next, conduct some research. Learn as much as you can about the topic and location you'll be guiding tours in. This will make your tours not only more informative but also more interesting. Captivating stories are the most important part of a successful tour. Next, remember that old adage: Practice makes perfect! Give tours to friends and family members before leading strangers. This will help you work out any kinks in your plan and give you more confidence when it's time to lead a real tour.

Finally, don't forget to promote your tours! Get the word out by posting flyers around town, talking to local businesses, and using social media. Be sure you cover all the pertinent details such as the language the tour is conducted in (don't make assumptions), the length and pace of the walk, and how long you expect the tour to take.

Get started! Even with a free tour, you may need permits and insurance. Be sure to check with your local chamber of commerce to determine local requirements. (toursbylocals.com)

Change a Child's Life

When you volunteer with the Foster Grandparent program, you have the opportunity to make a real difference in the lives of children in your community. As a mentor, you will provide support and guidance to help kids navigate the challenges of growing up. You'll also be a role model, showing them what it means to be a caring and responsible adult.

The Foster Grandparent program provides opportunities for seniors age fifty-five and older to share their time and talents with children in need. Volunteers can choose to work in a variety of settings, such as schools, Head Start centers, or hospitals. You might rock premature infants, teach the alphabet to preschool children, or tutor school-aged youth. For older children, you're serving as a mentor and role model, providing one-on-one attention and support.

The program is managed through partnerships between AmeriCorps and local organizations. You'll need to submit to a background check, and then you will be matched with a nonprofit near you to find the opportunity that best meets your preferences. The organization will provide training and ongoing support in this exciting endeavor.

In addition to making a positive impact on the children you mentor, you will also find volunteering with the Foster Grandparent program to be a rewarding experience for you. Spending time among children helps keep us young. You'll also gain satisfaction from knowing that you've made a difference in someone's life.

Get started! If you have at least five hours a week to dedicate to this important program, look for local opportunities at americorps.gov/serve/americorps-seniors.

Bring People Back from the Brink

When a disaster strikes, it can take months or even years for a community to recover. This is where volunteers like you come in. Organizations like All Hands and Hearts lead teams in providing disaster relief services to communities around the world. This organization has a wide range of programs that allow volunteers to get involved in everything from providing direct assistance to families in need to helping with long-term rebuilding efforts.

In the immediate aftermath of disasters, it deploys disaster assessment response teams to identify and prioritize immediate needs with local community leaders, lead quick-response units to clean up safety hazards, build short-term shelter, and establish water, sanitation, and hygiene facilities. Long-term projects include rebuilding schools and creating more permanent housing.

In addition to lending help to disaster recovery efforts after hurricanes, tornadoes, and earthquakes, All Hands and Hearts also has a year-round wildfire relief program in the western United States that creates fuel breaks and works with homeowners on removing damaged trees from their property as well as assisting with interior home restoration.

All Hands and Hearts is unique among other volunteer travel programs in that you don't need to pay a fee to attend. You only are required to cover the cost of your transportation. In addition, this isn't a typical voluntourism project with time for sightseeing. You'll work hard six days a week for two weeks to three months.

Get started! Learn more about becoming trained to serve on a disaster assessment response team or joining upcoming projects at allhandsandhearts.org.

Support Refugee Resettlement

The International Rescue Committee (IRC) is a global humanitarian organization that helps refugees who have been displaced by conflict or disaster. The IRC provides assistance with everything from finding shelter and food to providing medical care and psychological support. Volunteers play a vital role in the IRC's work, providing much-needed help to refugees who are struggling to rebuild their lives. There are many ways to get involved, from resettlement support in your local community to traveling to provide direct assistance in refugee camps.

There are currently twenty-six resettlement support offices in the United States and six in Europe that rely on volunteers to help provide critical services to refugees. Resettlement support volunteers serve on-call, assisting new refugee families who arrive in their local area. Tasks include helping families secure and furnish homes through donations with established partners. They also help families connect with interpreters and education advocates who will guide the families through the process of getting their children enrolled in school.

International volunteers sign up for more in-depth training and longer assignments (up to twelve months) to support the needs of displaced persons in refugee camps around the world. Primary services include education and childcare to unaccompanied children, vocational training for women, and medical care.

Get started! Learn more about how to become an IRC volunteer at rescue.org. You can see a listing of open positions with training requirements. Priority is given to people with experience, such as retired teachers and healthcare professionals.

CHAPTER FIVE

CHALLENGE YOURSELF

Retirement can be an exciting time to explore new things and visit new places. For many people, it's a time to finally pursue those interests they didn't have time for during their working years. Learning new things and exploring new locations can help keep your mind sharp and prevent boredom. It can also be a great way to meet new people and make new friends. Whether you're looking to learn a new language or take up a new hobby, retirement is the perfect time to challenge yourself and expand your horizons.

Unmask the Chinese Opera

Immerse yourself in an experience of acrobatics, drama, and distinctive music through this centuries-old form of theater. Traditionally, Chinese operas were performed in grand courtyards or temples, with the audience sitting on the ground to watch the show. Today, you can enjoy a spectacular opera performance in most cities across China. You'll be entranced by the brightly colored costumes and elaborate makeup of the performers. Don't worry if you don't know the language. The actors use exaggerated expressions and movements to tell the story, and theaters that cater to tourists provide English subtitles. Enjoying a performance is an unforgettable experience.

Get started! The Liyuan Theatre produces a performance daily. Learn more about the symbolism of the costume colors and masks at liyuantheatreopera.com/the-performance.

Plunge Like a Polar Bear

For many people, the thought of jumping into freezing cold water is enough to send a shiver down their spine. But for those brave souls willing to take the plunge, it's a once-in-a-lifetime adventure. In Alaska, there are numerous bodies of water across the state, each offering a unique experience. Choose from the vividly blue waters of the glaciers at Wrangell-St. Elias National Park & Preserve (the largest national park in the United States) or the bracing surf of the Arctic Ocean. If you're feeling especially adventurous, take a helicopter tour to a remote glacial pool.

Get started! Check out Tundra Tours (tundratoursinc.com/tours) in Barrow, Alaska, America's northernmost city, for a guided polar-bear plunge adventure in the Chukchi Sea (of the Arctic Ocean).

Travel with Strangers

Meeting new people is one of the best parts about travel. You get to learn about new cultures and customs, and you often form lifelong bonds with the people you meet. Unfortunately, it can be difficult to meet new people when you're traveling on your own. That's where tour groups come in. You'll have the opportunity to explore new cultures and see amazing places, all while bonding with fellow travelers. Many companies offer itineraries focusing on couples, solo travelers, and even family adventures with adult children. No matter what your interest is, there's a tour group out there for you.

Get started! Backroads (backroads.com) is a leader in the active travel tour space. With more than forty years in the business, it has the experience to make your group travel adventure one to remember.

Perfect Your Photo Skills

Iceland is a photographer's paradise. With its otherworldly landscapes and natural wonders, it's no wonder the country has become a popular destination for photographers from all over the world. To make the most out of your trip, join a tour whose guides will take you to all the best locations for shooting, whether you're interested in capturing glaciers, waterfalls, geysers, or the northern lights. Even better, because they're professionals, they'll be able to give you expert tips and advice on how to make the most of your camera equipment and get the best results possible.

Get started! Iceland Photo Tours (iceland-photo-tours.com) offers both group and private tours led by award-winning landscape photographers who know the country like the backs of their hands.

Behold Rare Birds in Papua New Guinea

If you have ever wanted to learn more about bird-watching, Papua New Guinea is the best place on earth to do it. Home to all but two of the forty-one birds of paradise as well as 900 other species of birds, it is a veritable wonderland for budding birders and experienced ornithologists alike.

On a tour of Papua New Guinea, you will have the opportunity to see some of the most amazing birds in the world, including the 103 species that can only be found on these islands, up close and personal. You will also learn about the different habitat types that these birds occupy as well as the threats they face. In addition, you will be able to share your love of birding with other like-minded individuals, making for an unforgettable experience.

Lindblad Expeditions has partnered with National Geographic to provide a more immersive and educational experience than you'll find with anyone else. With itineraries from thirteen to twenty-one days, you can explore some of the most remote and beautiful corners of Indonesia and Papua New Guinea while also learning about the importance of conservation. The partnership between Lindblad and National Geographic also allows for cutting-edge research and technology to be used on expeditions. This provides guests with an up-close look at the world around them while also allowing them to gain a deeper understanding of the importance of preserving our planet.

Get started! With more than fifty years as leaders in responsible tourism, Lindblad Expeditions strives to make a positive impact on the locations it visits. Learn more about its itineraries at expeditions.com/itineraries.

Tackle the Tiger's Nest

Paro Taktsang, also known as the Tiger's Nest, is one of the most unique and beautiful religious sites in the world. This spectacular monastery is perched on a cliff high over the Paro Valley in Bhutan, a small kingdom in the Himalayan Mountains. The stunning scenery and peaceful atmosphere make it a popular destination for both pilgrims and tourists alike.

Although the trip to the Tiger's Nest can be challenging, it is well worth the effort. You'll hike up 2.6 miles, gaining 1,707 feet of elevation along the way. It isn't extremely steep but is a gradual uphill climb. You'll start in a beautiful pine forest and pass colorful prayer flags. About halfway up, you can stop at a tea house to take a break for some refreshment. At that point, you'll continue up another mile to a viewpoint above the monastery where you can photograph it in all its glory.

Once you cross over to the monastery, you can take a tour of the grounds. Built around a series of caves in 1692, Tiger's Nest gets its name from the lore of Padmasambhava, who is credited with bringing Buddhism to Bhutan in the eighth century. It is said that he arrived at the mountaintop on a flying tiger.

Get started! The hike begins at 8,525 feet above sea level, and the altitude has been known to cause discomfort in some. Be sure to acclimate before you start this activity.

Participate in an Epic Pilgrimage

The Camino de Santiago (the Way of Saint James) is a centuries-old series of routes that span France, Portugal, and Spain, ending in Santiago de Compostela in northern Spain. Every year, thousands of people from all over the world embark on the Camino, each with their own reasons for undertaking such a journey. For some, it is a religious pilgrimage; for others, it is a way to challenge themselves physically and mentally.

Regardless of why you choose to walk the Camino de Santiago, there are certain benefits that everyone can enjoy. With most walkers covering an average of ten miles per day, one of the most obvious benefits is physical exercise. The scenic routes and tranquil villages provide a much-needed respite from the noise and pollution of urban areas. Finally, the Camino is a great opportunity to meet new people from all over the world. Whether you are bonding over shared struggles or simply sharing stories around a campfire, you are sure to make lasting connections with your fellow pilgrims.

One of the great things about this trek is that you can choose to walk as little or as much as you want. If you only want to traverse a portion of it, there are numerous options available. The French Way, the most popular route, is more strenuous as it begins in the Pyrenees, while the Portuguese Way is easier as it follows the relatively flat but dramatic Atlantic coastline.

Get started! Caminoways.com will help you customize the right trek for you, including hotel stays, daily luggage transfers, and more.

Swim on the Edge of Victoria Falls

Perched on top of one of the world's most magnificent waterfalls, Devil's Pool is a naturally formed rock pool with a view to remember. Although the name makes it sound dangerous, there is no need to worry as there is a ledge around the pool that will prevent swimmers from being pulled over the edge of Victoria Falls. In addition, you can only access the pool with a guide who is skilled at assessing current conditions. If you still don't want to take the risk you can enjoy the view from a safe distance and observe the more adventurous take a dip in the refreshing waters.

Located on the Zambezi River, Victoria Falls is the largest waterfall in Africa and one of the Seven Natural Wonders of the World. Standing over a mile wide and 354 feet high, it is truly a sight to behold. Once you've experienced the view from the top, there is still much more to see of this natural marvel.

Bordering two countries, Victoria Falls consists of five falls. Four are located in Zimbabwe: Devil's Cataract, Horseshoe Falls, Main Falls, and Rainbow Falls. Eastern Cataract is in Zambia. Both sides are protected by national parks and have spectacular views of the falls. In addition, Zambezi National Park, just three miles southwest of the falls, is home to a host of wildlife such as antelopes, cape buffalo, elephants, giraffes, lions, and zebras.

Get started! Devil's Pool is only open during the dry season (mid-August to mid-January) based on safe water levels. Book with a reputable tour company at livingstoneisland.com to ensure a safe trip.

Brave Being Bilingual

A great way to enhance your travels is to learn a foreign language, and there's no better way to do that than to immerse yourself in the culture and attend a language program abroad. These short-term intensive language schools offer you the ability to learn a language in a short period of time by providing opportunities to surround yourself with it.

Lingua Service Worldwide, an independent agency that recommends language schools around the world, visits and assesses them to ensure that you will receive a quality experience. Recognizing the challenges of learning a language later in life, it identifies programs it feels are best suited to adults over age fifty so you can take advantage of your retirement to explore the world and improve your language skills.

While attending an immersion language program, you'll not only receive expert instruction from native speakers, but you'll also have the opportunity to practice what you've learned in real-world settings. A tutor will take you on guided group shopping excursions, museum tours, and dinners. Finally, you'll have two options for lodging: a local hotel or a host family stay, with the latter being recommended for maximum learning potential.

Because Lingua Service Worldwide recommends programs in locations all over the world, you can choose a destination that appeals to your interests. For example, you can choose to learn Spanish in Spain or South America and French in Belgium, Canada, or France.

Get started! To get the most out of your immersion program, start with a smartphone or tablet app like Duolingo or Babbel to learn the basics.

Trace Your Heritage

Your family roots are an essential part of who you are. Learning about your genealogy can help you understand your identity and where you come from. Tracing your ancestry can be a time-consuming but rewarding task. Understanding where you come from can give you a sense of self-worth and belonging. You are unique, and your family history is a big part of what makes you special.

A good place to begin tracing your heritage is by talking to your relatives to see what information they have about your family. If you don't have many living relatives or if they don't know much about your family history, you can try looking through old family photos and documents to see if you can find any clues there. Another option is to take an ancestry DNA test. This will give you more information about your genetic makeup and can help you connect with distant relatives who might be able to tell you more about your family history. You can also use genealogy websites to research your ancestry. These websites can be a great resource for finding information about your ancestors and connecting with other people who are researching the same thing.

Use your newfound knowledge to embrace your culture and celebrate family traditions. You may even choose to travel to your ancestral lands.

Get started! Ancestry.com has various levels of membership that allow you to take a DNA test, create family trees, and search for information from the census and other government sources.

Learn the Art of Aviation

For many people, flying a plane is the ultimate dream. The freedom of the open skies, the wind in your hair, and the thrill of piloting a complex machine—what could be better? Although it may seem like a daunting task, learning to fly a plane can be an immensely rewarding experience. Not only will you gain a unique skill set, but you'll also enjoy unparalleled views of the world around you. And who knows—maybe one day you'll even find yourself flying to far-flung destinations.

A terrific option with lower barriers to entry is the sport pilot certificate. It was created in 2004 with the goal of making aviation more accessible to the general public. Compared to the traditional private pilot certificate, sport pilots receive the same privileges but are restricted to flying lighter two-seat aircraft during the day. This makes the training process cheaper and faster without sacrificing safety. In addition, sport pilots are not required to obtain an FAA medical certificate, making it even easier for people to get into aviation.

One thing that is surprising to many about flight school is that you learn a lot more than simply how to operate the aircraft. There are so many other aspects involved in this pursuit, such as flight planning, navigation systems, and weather.

Get started! If you haven't already, take a demonstration flight to see how it feels to be in the cockpit. Next, find a reputable flight school from the Aircraft Owners and Pilots Association's free online directory (aopa.org/learntofly).

Luge at Utah's Olympic Park

The bobsled experience at the Olympic Park in Salt Lake City, Utah, will take you on an unforgettable ride. This was the official sliding track used in the 2002 Winter Olympics for the bobsled, luge, and skeleton events. Now you have the chance to speed down the ice like so many athletes since the first Winter Olympics in 1924. Today, this is a year-round activity. In the winter, you'll speed down the ice with one of the park's professional pilots. In the summer, you'll ride in a modified bobsled that races down the track's concrete surface.

This experience is not for the faint of heart. Participants should be prepared for a wild ride! In just under one minute, you'll race down the 0.83-mile track with fifteen turns as you descend 340 feet. The excitement starts as you accelerate immediately, reaching speeds up to 80 miles per hour and experiencing five Gs of force. Although it is an extreme ride, every effort has been made to ensure your safety. You'll get a safety orientation and be outfitted with a helmet and seat belt.

While you're at the park, be sure to take time to explore. It is still a training center for Olympic athletes. You can take a guided tour of the training facility, watch a freestyle show performed by these athletes, and even learn to use the freestyle jump ramp.

Get started! This is one of only a few places in the world where you can participate in this thrilling activity. Be sure to purchase your tickets well in advance at utaholympiclegacy.org.

Host a Homestay

Meeting people from other cultures can be a truly eye-opening experience. Although their customs and beliefs may be different from your own, making these connections is a great way to recognize our shared humanity. Dublin-based homestay.com runs a program that is a step up from couch surfing. In this case, you rent out a room to international travelers for a small fee. Although you aren't required to serve as a tour guide, you may choose to invite your guests to activities to allow them to gain a better understanding of your local area. The point of the program isn't to save money but to have a deeper connection to a destination. In fact, most of the people who have used the program are over the age of thirty-five and just over 20 percent are age fifty and above.

In addition to homestay.com, many local university and language programs are always looking for new homestay hosts to allow their students a chance to experience American life firsthand and practice their language skills with native speakers.

These programs are also a wonderful opportunity to learn about new ways of life and to find common ground with someone from a different background. By opening up your home and inviting others in, you can create a space where cultural exchange can take place.

Get started! Register as a host with homestay.com, and you will be matched with a local partner organization. You can specify what dates you're available and whether you want to host students, singles, couples, or families.

Walk High in the Sky

If you're seeking out truly spectacular views, there's no better way to find them than by crossing some of the world's most unique pedestrian bridges. These bridges are designed specifically for pedestrians, which means you can walk high above dramatic gorges, lush forests, raging seas, and even between mountain peaks.

One of the most dramatic viewpoints of North America's iconic Grand Canyon is from the Skywalk. This cantilevered glass bridge extends seventy feet out from the canyon wall, providing visitors with breathtaking views of the canyon below. Extended 4,000 feet above the canyon's floor, the skywalk is located on the Hualapai Tribe's reservation. The walk itself is just under a mile long, and there are several lookout points along the way.

Ireland's Carrick-a-Rede Rope Bridge may not be one of the highest pedestrian bridges, but dangling more than 300 feet over the rocky sea below, it can sure be one of the scariest to traverse. The knotted rope bridge links the mainland to the tiny island of Carrick-a-Rede and has been in use for more than 350 years by salmon fishermen.

Spanning nearly 500 feet, Switzerland's Trift Bridge presents sweeping vistas of the Swiss Alps. But what makes the Trift Bridge truly special is its location. Perched above a turquoise blue glacial lake more than 330 feet below, it can only be reached by cable car and an hour-and-a-half hike.

Get started! Pedestrian bridges have long been a popular means of attracting tourists to a scenic region. This article lists several in the United States: onlyinyourstate.com/usa/swinging-bridges-usa.

Book It Back to School

It's never too late to learn something new. That's especially true for adults looking to challenge themselves in retirement. In fact, a study by the University of Pennsylvania surveyed a group of retirees who had all returned to school, and the vast majority of respondents reported feeling more fulfilled as a result. In addition to providing mental stimulation, it can also be a great way to pursue a long-held passion or simply try something new.

Many universities across the United States even offer free courses to seniors in their communities. If you skipped your desire to major in medieval literature for a more practical degree, now may be the time to go back and do it. The Osher Lifelong Learning Institute partners with universities to support mature adults who are seeking the joy of learning without the need for a degree.

Traditional coursework isn't the only option, either. Have you always wanted to learn how to make the perfect soufflé or decorate elaborate cakes? You might want to consider a local culinary school. You don't need to enroll in a full program geared at a job in the industry. Most offer weekend workshops and short courses. Local community colleges and recreation centers also host courses on a wide range of topics, from computers and smartphone technology to photography and woodworking.

Get started! Decide what you want to learn, and then seek out information on available programs from your public library, community college, or recreation center. This article provides additional ideas: https://seniors.lovetoknow.com/ Free_Senior_Citizen_Education.

Appreciate Ancient Artifacts

Composed of twenty-one museums, galleries, and zoos, the Smithsonian Institution in Washington, D.C., is home to some of the most revered museums in the world, and best of all, entry is free! Visitors can explore exhibits on art, history, science, and culture from all over the world. Highlights include the National Museum of African American History and Culture, the National Air and Space Museum, and the American Art Museum.

One of the best things about these museums is the guided tours offering insights into the collections. Most of the museums are so vast, it would be hard to really appreciate what they offer without an overview. For example, with more than 350,000 square feet of public display space, the Smithsonian National Museum of Natural History houses the world's largest collection of natural history artifacts, spread over three floors of exhibit halls.

If you're interested in Indigenous American history, the five-story National Museum of the American Indian is one of the largest and most diverse museums in the world. It boasts a collection of more than 800,000 artifacts, photographs, and documents representing the more than 1,200 Indigenous cultures throughout the Americas. The museum is filled with multimedia displays laid out by geographical regions and tribal communities.

The Smithsonian also has a lot of outdoor displays, such as the Smithsonian Castle's memorial gardens, the Hirshhorn Sculpture Garden, and the 163-acre National Zoo.

Get started! Learn more about the Smithsonian complex at si.edu /visit. Some of the museums require timed-entry reservations, which can book up quickly during peak holidays and summer.

Take the Stage at TEDx

Share your knowledge with others through the power of public speaking. Founded in 1984 at a conference on the convergence of technology, entertainment, and design, TED has become an international powerhouse devoted to sharing ideas. In addition to the large stage, TEDx events are held in communities throughout the world.

The goal of TEDx events is to share ideas and spark critical conversations locally. They don't focus on one specific topic but instead foster inspiration through a wide range of subjects. There aren't many rules, but it is important to note that TEDx events aren't used to promote specific religious or political affiliations. Any science or health information must be supported by peer-reviewed research.

If you're thinking of getting up on that famous red dot and sharing your great ideas, here are a few things to keep in mind. First, remember that a TED Talk is all about storytelling. Think about a personal story you can share that will resonate with your audience. Second, focus on delivering your message with clarity and passion. The goal is to connect with your audience on an emotional level, so make sure your body language and facial expressions convey the energy and excitement of your talk. Finally, don't be afraid to add a little humor. A well-placed joke can help break the ice and endear you to your audience.

Get started! The TED Talks website (ted.com) has many videos on how to improve your speaking technique. Toastmasters International (toastmasters.org) has a network of clubs that teach public speaking skills.

Find Your *Fahrenheit 451*

Every year, thousands of books are banned from schools and libraries around the world. In most cases, banning books comes down to three main reasons: offensive language, sexually explicit content, and violence. Of course, not everyone agrees on what qualifies as offensive or explicit, which is why these decisions are often controversial.

Even books that have been widely praised can end up on the chopping block. For example, soon after it was published, Harper Lee's Pulitzer Prize–winning novel *To Kill a Mockingbird* was banned in many school districts in the United States for its use of racially charged language. Today, it remains one of the most frequently challenged books in the country. Ray Bradbury's *Fahrenheit 451*, a book about censorship inspired by the McCarthy era, has often been banned for pushing an agenda.

As adults, it's important for us to read banned books before passing judgment upon them. By reading a banned book, we can gain insight into different cultures and viewpoints. What's more, reading banned books can also help us learn about the history of censorship and the importance of defending our right to freedom of speech. Given the power of literature to inspire change and promote understanding, it is important to protect our right to read freely and openly. Otherwise, we risk censoring the stories that need to be told.

Get started! The American Library Association keeps an extensive list of banned and challenged books in the United States. It also hosts a Banned Books Week each fall. Learn more at ala.org /advocacy/bbooks.

Know the Nautical Necessities

There's something about the freedom of sailing that attracts millions of people to the open water each year. As you move away from the shores, you become one with the wind and water surrounding you. Whether you prefer the calm of a lake or the thrill of the seas, learning to sail will open a lifetime of adventures to you.

The best way to learn to sail is to take lessons from a qualified instructor. This way, you get one-on-one attention and are able to ask questions as you learn the basics of sailing. You'll also be able to practice on your own time so that when you're out on the water, you'll be confident in your abilities.

As you can imagine, sailing is dependent on the wind. As a result, you'll spend a lot of time learning about wind conditions and how they affect your sails. You'll also need to know how to tack, or turn the boat into the wind, to change direction. Finally, you need to be able to read nautical charts to navigate your way around obstacles. Of course, safety is emphasized with each lesson. You'll typically start with small boats less than twenty-five feet in length, which can easily be handled by one person. You'll be able to master the concepts quickly and can apply them to larger sailboats later if you so desire.

Get started! The American Sailing Association has more than 400 schools that all teach a standardized curriculum. Find one near you at asa.com/find-sailing-school.

Perform in Public

Share in the joy of making someone else smile by participating in a flash mob. Although the word "mob" sounds a little sinister, this activity is anything but. A flash mob is a group of people who assemble suddenly in a public place to perform for a brief time and then quickly disperse.

These events are quick and quirky and often involve music, song, and dance to bring a smile to those who witness them. Imagine walking down a busy street near a park on your way to a meeting and seeing someone break out in dance. Then a few others join him and are quickly joined by a few more until it becomes a group of seemingly unrelated people dancing in public.

Participating in a flash mob is a great way to spread some happiness, and the best part about a flash mob is that anyone can join in—you don't need any special skills or training. All you need is a positive attitude and a willingness to have some fun. Bruno Mars's song "Marry You" has become a favorite flash mob proposal tool since its release in 2010. Flash mobs using the song typically follow a simple line dance; you can learn the dance online in advance and just join in the fun.

Get started! The best way to find out about a flash mob is to use social media networks and type in the keywords "flash mob" to find one near you. There's even an organization, Flash Mob America (flashmobamerica.com), that produces these fun events around the country.

Get Hooked on Geocaching

If you're looking for a fun and interesting way to spend time outdoors, then you should learn about this simple type of treasure hunt. With geocaching, you use GPS coordinates to pinpoint the location of a hidden cache. Geocaching started in May 2000, and there are now more than 2.5 million caches worldwide.

The waterproof cache containers range from micro, small, and medium to large. Micro containers are just large enough for a small rolled-up sheet of paper to serve as a log, and the large containers are bigger than a shoebox. Individuals hide them on their property (or on public property with permission) and typically include a log and swag—small prizes like stickers or small toys. The only rule is that if you take a piece of swag, you should leave something in return for the next person. The true prize for adult participants is finding the cache!

The official geocaching website uses a five-star scale for difficulty, factoring in size of the cache and the terrain that needs to be traversed to find it. For example, a one-star (easy) cache might be easily accessible in a local park and the size of a shoebox. Difficult caches might be camouflaged microcontainers that require a difficult hike or even a swim to find. There are even multicaches with hidden coordinates at each step to guide you along the way.

Get started! Create a free account on geocaching.com to find a cache in your area. The simplest way to navigate is to use the smartphone app, but you can also print the coordinates and hints.

Support the Arts

Community theater provides a unique and magical experience for both the performers and the audience. There is something special about live theater that cannot be replicated in any other form of entertainment. For the performers and theater crew, it is a chance to tell a story and to connect with an audience in a positive way. For the audience, community theater provides an opportunity to see their friends and neighbors in a completely different light. More than anything, the theater allows everyone the opportunity to lose themselves in another world for a couple of hours and to escape the stresses of everyday life.

Most community theaters put on two to four plays per year and are run entirely by volunteers. Whether you want to be onstage or behind the scenes, there is a role for you. In fact, even if you'd like to perform, starting in another capacity is a good way to get to know everyone involved and see how the company operates. From set building and costume design to selling tickets and ushering, there are more roles to fill than there are volunteers in most cases. Regardless of your specific duties, have a positive attitude and, above all, be reliable. Those two traits will go a long way toward making any production a success.

Get started! Find a local theater near you by typing "community theater near me" in a search engine. If the theater doesn't have a website, call or see if it has a Facebook page.

Find Your Inner Zen

Tai chi is an ancient Chinese practice that involves slow, flowing movements and deep breathing. It is often described as "meditation in motion" because it is believed to promote inner peace and harmony. Retirement is a great time to take up this practice, particularly for the physical and emotional health benefits.

Practicing tai chi can help improve balance, flexibility, and strength. This makes it very complementary to other forms of exercise, as it can significantly help with recovery. The improved balance is especially important to retirees as we age and are at increased risk of falling. Tai chi can also help reduce stress, anxiety, and depression. In addition, it has been shown to improve sleep quality and boost energy levels.

One of the best things about tai chi is that anyone can do it, from the most fit to those with mobility issues. And you don't need specific equipment, just loose, comfortable clothing. The practice includes 103 movements, called forms, that are coupled with breathing exercises. You don't need to learn them all at once; just start with a few and get in the groove. Once you've done it for a couple of weeks, you should begin to feel some of the benefits, which is a great encouragement to keep going. Although you don't need to practice tai chi with a group, it is a great way to get feedback on your form.

Get Started! Many community rec centers offer free group tai chi sessions. There are also numerous tutorials on YouTube that make it easy to practice at home.

Get Serious about Scuba

Have you ever dreamed of floating weightlessly like an astronaut, investigating unusual species like a field researcher, or looking for lost objects like a treasure hunter? If so, then learning to scuba dive may be for you! Scuba diving is a unique experience that allows you to explore the underwater world in a way that is not possible on land. Whether you want to explore reefs or shipwrecks or simply see the amazing variety of fish that inhabit the oceans, diving is an experience you will never forget. In addition, diving is a great way to meet new people and make friends who share your passion for the underwater world.

Most important, it is very simple to learn the basics of diving. The only prerequisite is the ability to swim. You need to be able to swim 300 yards in a mask with a snorkel and fins. You also have to tread water and float for ten minutes. The course itself starts with an in-person or online class that covers the basic theory of scuba diving. The second step is to complete a series of pool dives, which will allow you to get comfortable with the equipment and practice basic safety procedures. The third step is to complete an open water dive, which allows you to experience the sensation of diving in the ocean. Once you have completed these steps, you will be officially certified as a scuba diver.

Get started! The Professional Association of Diving Instructors has courses around the world. Find one near you at locator.padi.com.

Become Medieval Royalty

Renaissance fairs are a great way to experience history firsthand. From the moment you step through the gates, you are transported back in time to a world of knights and ladies, jesters and troubadours. If you attend a large Renaissance fair, you'll be astounded by the number of activities. For instance, the Maryland Renaissance Festival has ten stages with a wide range of performances from more than 200 entertainers. Whether you're watching a jousting tournament, laughing at jesters, gaping in awe at acrobats, or listening to minstrels sing, you'll feel like you've stepped into another age.

Renaissance fairs offer more than just entertainment; they also provide an opportunity to learn about life in medieval times. With the fair typically laid out like an ancient village, you can watch artisans working with glass or metal, try your hand at archery and axe throwing, or simply enjoy the sights and sounds of a bygone era. Don't forget to try some fantastic food and drinks.

You don't have to wear a costume, although doing so can make the experience more fun. Most of the large Renaissance fairs occur over a series of weekends, typically for six to eight weeks, and have vendors that sell and rent costumes, so go ahead and wear regular clothes the first time, and if you like it enough to go back, check out the costume vendors or make your own!

Get started! Find a Renaissance fair near you at therenlist.com or travel to one of the premiere fairs in the United States in Arizona (arizona.renfestinfo.com), Maryland (rennfest.com), or Minnesota (renaissancefest.com).

Be an Accidental Tourist

There's something special about an unplanned trip. Without the weight of expectation, you're free to simply enjoy the journey. Every turn is a surprise, and every destination an unexpected treat. Instead of ticking items off a list, you're allowed to simply go with the flow. In many ways, it's the perfect way to travel.

For starters, you could decide to take a trip and not choose the destination until the last minute. If it's a road trip, you could choose to drive in a specific direction and see what you discover along the way. If you're flying, log on to an airline's website and see what flights are on sale. If you're worried about finding accommodation, go to a booking website like Expedia and find a last-minute package deal. By leaving your itinerary open-ended, you give yourself the opportunity to follow your nose and see where the wind takes you. You might end up in some place you never would have thought to visit, and that's half the fun.

An unplanned road trip in your own state can be especially fun. You have the comfort of knowing at least a little of the region, but with the ability to branch out and find unexpected towns and attractions along the way. Even the smallest towns have tourist bureaus or chambers of commerce that tout their highlights.

Get started! The most important part of an unplanned trip is your budget. Luckily, last-minute flights and accommodations are often on sale if you are willing to go with the flow.

Migrate with the Seasons

Have you ever wished you could fly south for the winter or head to cooler climes in the summer? It might not be as hard as you think. With home rental services like Airbnb and Vrbo, it is fairly simple to find a rental for a few weeks or even a few months. You'll want to be sure to conduct some research before you pick a location. Even within a specific state, there can be a wide range of climate zones. For example, many snowbirds think of the desert as a great winter destination, but places like Flagstaff and Sedona, Arizona, are at a higher elevation and may be a better option to escape the heat in the summer.

Once you have an idea of the general region where you'd like to stay, consider your budget to narrow down the precise location. The Florida beaches are fairly pricey year-round, but some less so than others. The Daytona Beach area on the Atlantic Coast and the Pensacola Beach area on the Gulf Coast are much more affordable than Miami or the Florida Keys.

If you have an RV, staying at a campground can be an even better option. You can choose one to fit your preferences, from a nature-based campground near a state or national park to an RV resort on a golf course—and everything in between.

Get started! Peruse sites like Airbnb (airbnb.com) and Vrbo (vrbo.com) to find fully furnished rentals. Campendium.com is a great site to find campgrounds if you have an RV.

Fly from the Mountaintops

If you'd like to challenge yourself to an adrenaline-pumping adventure, then look no further than the world's longest zip line in Ras Al Khaimah, United Arab Emirates. Measuring in at 1.75 miles, this zip line will send you flying over the desert landscape at speeds up to ninety miles per hour. There is even a double line, so if you're there with a friend or significant other, you can race side by side at the same time!

Beyond the rush of the ride, you will experience some of the most incredible views. Your flight begins from the top of the Jebal Jais mountains at just over 5,500 feet above sea level. You're strapped in to fly like Superman, facedown and head first; you will truly have a bird's-eye view of the mountainous terrain and deep valleys. As you near the end of the ride, you'll pause on a glass-bottomed platform 262 feet from the ground before completing the final half mile to the end.

If you didn't have enough fun, the adventure park also features the region's longest toboggan ride, the Jais Sledder, as well as a series of six zip lines known as the Jais Sky Tour. The toboggan ride is like a two-seat roller coaster that travels more than 6,000 feet down the mountainside. You have a break that allows you to set the speed topping out at close to twenty-five miles per hour, which at that elevation seems faster than it sounds!

Get started! Learn more about the activities in the area as well as lodging and restaurants at visitrasalkhaimah.com/plan-your-trip.

Soar through the Sky

There's nothing quite like the feeling of soaring high above a city, taking in the breathtaking views while feeling the rush of the wind in your face. If you're looking for an unforgettable adventure, look no further than tandem hang gliding over Rio de Janeiro. Not only will you get to experience the city from a unique perspective, but you'll also be able to enjoy views of some of Rio's most iconic landmarks, including the ninety-eight-foot Christ the Redeemer statue, Sugarloaf Mountain rising out of the Atlantic Ocean, and the jagged Dois Irmãos (two brothers) rock formation.

Best of all, you'll be in a tandem hang glider with a professional pilot. You'll both be attached to the glider with a harness, with the passenger at an elevated position just above the pilot. You will marvel at the view while the pilot manages the controls.

More than 30,000 tandem hang-gliding flights occur each year in Rio. Takeoffs are usually done from the Pedra Bonita ramp in Tijuca National Park. All it takes is ten to twelve running steps off the edge of a platform that is a little over 1,600 feet above the sea below and you're aloft! Once airborne, the pilot uses thermal currents to keep the glider airborne while also steering it toward a landing area.

Get started! Find a reputable hang-gliding operator with certified pilots by reading reviews on tripadvisor.com. Learn more about the process and watch videos of previous tours at riohanggliding.com.

Walk around Germany

Volksmarching is a fun and noncompetitive way to get outside and enjoy the fresh air. Introduced in Germany in the late 1960s, the term *volksmarsch* means "people's march." Today, there are more than forty recognized clubs around the world that organize events under the International Federation of Popular Sports (IVV). But why not go to its birthplace to experience this fun way to see some of the country on foot?

Organized walks are set for a range of distances, most often 3.1 miles (5 kilometers), 6.2 miles (10 kilometers), 9.3 miles (15 kilometers), and 12.4 miles (20 kilometers). These are held at specific dates and times and provide the advantage of meeting new people and earning a pin for your walking stick or rain jacket.

If you don't want to be constrained by the calendar or simply prefer solitude on your jaunts, the IVV has recognized hundreds of permanent walking routes in a variety of distances. They can be on a wide range of terrain from urban to mountainous but are always rated to show the difficulty. They are also well marked with signs or painted blazes on trees if the path is outside the city.

If you join a local volksmarching club, you'll get access to logbooks and procedures for submitting all walks you've completed during your travels. Then you can participate anywhere and earn awards that serve as great mementos of your adventures on foot.

For another Germany destination, see page 34.

Get started! Learn more about volksmarching and find routes around the world at ivv-online.org/walking-worldwide.html. Try one out close to home, and then plan to complete a few on your travels.

RESOURCES

CHAPTER ONE

Corcovado National Park
costa-rica-guide.com/nature/national-parks/corcovado

Visit Dubai
visitdubai.com/en/places-to-visit/palm-jumeirah-2

Hurtigruten Galápagos Expeditions
hurtigruten.com/destinations/galapagos-islands/galapagos-islands
-expedition-in-darwins-footsteps

Guide to the Great Barrier Reef
australia.com/en-us/places/cairns-and-surrounds/guide-to-the-great
-barrier-reef.html

Tulum Visitors Guide
islandlifemexico.com/tulum-visitors-guide

Great Serengeti Wildebeest Migration Guide
africanmeccasafaris.com/travel-guide/tanzania/parks-reserves
/serengeti/wildebeest-migration

National Geographic Explorer
expeditions.com/about/fleet/national-geographic-explorer

Intrepid Great Wall of China Tours
intrepidtravel.com/us/china/great-wall-of-china-from-beijing

Osprey Expeditions Angel Falls Tour
ospreyexpeditions.com/angel-falls-orinoco

Tivoli, Italian Department of Culture and Tourism
visittivoli.eu/le-ville/villa-d-este&lang=EN

Arctic Adventures Ice Cave Excursions
adventures.is/iceland/day-tours/ice-caves

Horse Riding Holidays Kyrgyzstan Steppe Tour

bookhorseridingholidays.com/novi-nomad/6-day-fantastic-horse
-riding-tour-in-kyrgyzstan

Discover Old Town Warsaw

warsawtour.pl/en/project/old-town-2

Wild Frontiers Travel Great Silk Road Adventure

wildfrontierstravel.com/en_GB/destination/china/group-tours
/the-great-silk-road-adventure-xian-to-istanbul/gsr

National Parks of Japan, Aso-Kuju

https://www.japan.travel/national-parks/parks/aso-kuju/

CHAPTER TWO

Cookly Fish Market Experience

cookly.me/do/1562-sushi-experience-shop-fish-market-sushi-making
/in/tokyo

Kyoto-Uji Tour

viator.com/tours/uji/kyoto-uji-matcha-and-byodo-in-temple
-walking-tour/d50678-63670P47

Stadtmaus Weltenburg Brewery Tour

stadtmaus.de/rund-ums-bier/brauereifuehrungen-weltenburg.html
#regiondo-2022-05-14

The Danube Narrows

bavariandaytours.com/other-great-destinations/danube-narrows

La Morra Truffle Hunting Experience

viator.com/tours/langhe-roero-and-monferrato/la-morra-truffle
-hunting-tour-experience/d25960-150511P3

Greece Real Food Adventure

intrepidtravel.com/us/greece/greece-real-food-adventure-124485

Marrakech Cooking Class

viator.com/tours/marrakech/experience-morocco-visit-a-souq
-and-cook-a-tagine-in-marrakech/d5408-6057tagine

Brussels Chocolate Tour

globalenterprises.be/tour/brussels-chocolate-tour

Lapland Hotels Snow Village

laplandhotels.com/EN/hotels-in-lapland/yllas/lapland-hotels
-snowvillage/restaurants.html

Soneva Resorts Treepod Dining

soneva.com/resorts/soneva-kiri/dining

Traveling Spoon Vietnamese Cooking Class

travelingspoon.com/hosts/2575-traditional-vietnamese-cuisine
-with-maia

Amman Street Food Walking Tour

viator.com/en-AU/tours/amman/private-street-food-and-walking
-tour-amman-downtown/d5503-107508P3

Polish Vodka Tour with Locals

withlocals.com/experience/for-the-love-of-polish-alcohol-tastings
-culture-c16d91f8

Whisky Tours of Scotland

rabbies.com/en/scotland-tours/see/whisky-tours-scotland

Blandy's Wine Lodge

blandyswinelodge.com/tours

Sacred Valley Picnic Experience

peru.travel/en/experiences/picnic-in-the-sacred-valley

Turkish Coffee Making Tour

afiyetolsunistanbul.com/turkish-tea-coffee-making-tasting-tour

Food Fantastique

foodfantastique.ca/dining-on-the-ocean-floor

CHAPTER THREE

Casa de Arbol

atlasobscura.com/places/swing-at-the-end-of-the-world

Blue Hawaiian Helicopter Tours

bluehawaiian.com/en/bigisland/tours/big-island-spectacular

Skylodge Adventure Suites

naturavive.com/web/skylodge-adventure-suites

Lake Louise Ski Resort

skilouise.com/activities/winter-fun/snowshoe-tours/scenic
-showshoe-tour

International Dark-Sky Association

darksky.org/our-work/conservation/idsp/finder

Hawk Conservancy

hawk-conservancy.org/your-visit/experiences/a-day-with-birds
-of-prey

Love the Maldives

lovethemaldives.com/guide-swimming-sharks-maldives

Engholm Lodge Husky Sledding

magneticnorthtravel.com/tour/details/husky-sledding-from-engholm
-lodge-five-day-tour

Bora Bora Travel Guide

tahiti.com/island/bora-bora

Fjord Norway

fjordnorway.com/en/inspiration/the-best-fjord-cruises-in-fjord
-norway

Powwow Primer

powwows.com/main/native-american-pow-wow

Mongolia Travel News

toursmongolia.com/mongolia_travel_news/what-to-know-about
-naadam-festival-before-you-attend

Namibia Wildlife Resorts

nwr.com.na/resorts/sossus-dune-lodge

Mount Kilimanjaro National Park Day Trip

getyourguide.com/moshi-l32320/mount-kilimanjaro-national-park
-day-trip-t386536

Sea Quest Kayak

sea-quest-kayak.com/kayaking-san-juan-islands/washington-whale
-watching-seattle

Klondike Experience

klondikeexperience.com/summer-tour/city-and-goldfields

Klondike Visitors Association

klondikevisitorsassociation.ca/free-claim-6

516 Arouca Bridge Tour

getyourguide.com/516-arouca-suspension-bridge-l170132

CHAPTER FOUR

Relay For Life

cancer.org/involved/fundraise/relay-for-life.html

Iracambi

iracambi.com/projects/forests-4-water

Earthwatch Archaeology Project

earthwatch.org/expeditions/discovering-ancient-societies-portugal

All Out Africa Whale Shark Conservation

alloutafrica.com/volunteer-projects/conservation-projects/marine
-research-and-whale-shark-conservation-volunteer-project

Colonial Williamsburg

colonialwilliamsburg.org

The Henry Ford

thehenryford.org/about/employment/volunteering

National Park Service Adopt a Trail

nps.gov/pete/getinvolved/adopt-a-trail.htm

Cookies for Kids' Cancer

cookiesforkidscancer.org/pages/fundraising

Earthwatch Pollinators Project

earthwatch.org/expeditions/conserving-wild-bees-and-other
-pollinators-of-costa-rica

Earthwatch South Africa Rhino Conservation

earthwatch.org/expeditions/conserving-threatened-rhinos-in
-south-africa

AmeriCorps Foster Grandparent Program

americorps.gov/serve/fit-finder/americorps-seniors-foster
-grandparent-program

CHAPTER FIVE

National Geographic Papua New Guinea

nationalgeographic.com/travel/destination/papua-new-guinea

National Geographic Bhutan

nationalgeographic.com/expeditions/destinations/asia/land/bhutan

Lingua Service Worldwide

linguaserviceworldwide.com/language-courses-for-seniors

Aircraft Owners and Pilots Association

aopa.org/training-and-safety/learn-to-fly/flying-for-fun

Flying **Magazine**

flyingmag.com/learn-to-fly-sport-pilot-certificate

Organize a Local TEDx Event

ted.com/participate/organize-a-local-tedx-event

Acknowledgments

First, I must thank my husband, Sean, for his steadfast support in all my writing endeavors, including this one. He is my biggest cheerleader and the person who convinced me to become a writer. He's always the voice of reason when I overcommit myself (again and again), and I wouldn't accomplish much without him in my corner.

Many thanks also to my crew—Julie, Kim, Laurie, and Mindy—for encouraging me to push myself physically and mentally. You're always a source of inspiration to me.

About the Author

 Julie Chickery is a travel writer and public speaker. After both serving twenty years in the U.S. Air Force, Julie and her husband lived and traveled full-time in an RV for six years. Learn more about her travel adventures at chickerystravels.com.